MW01243056

**John Buchan** was born in
Childhood holidays were spent in the Borders, for which he had a
great love. His passion for the Scottish countryside is reflected in
his writing. He was educated at Glasgow University and Brasenose
College, Oxford, where he was President of the Union.

Called to the Bar in 1901, he became Lord Milner's assistant
private secretary in South Africa. In 1907 he was a publisher with
Nelson's. In World War I he was a *Times* correspondent at the
Front, an officer in the Intelligence Corps and adviser to the War
Cabinet. He was elected Conservative MP in one of the Scottish
Universities' seats in 1927 and was created Baron Tweedsmuir in
1935. From 1935 until his death in 1940 he was Governor
General of Canada.

Buchan is most famous for his adventure stories. High in
romance, these are peopled by a large cast of characters, of which
Richard Hannay is his best known. Hannay appears in *The Thirty-
nine Steps*. Alfred Hitchcock adapted it for the screen. A TV series
featured actor Robert Powell as Richard Hannay.

**FICTION**

THE BLANKET OF THE DARK
CASTLE GAY
THE COURTS OF THE MORNING
THE DANCING FLOOR
THE FREE FISHERS
THE GAP IN THE CURTAIN
GREENMANTLE
GREY WEATHER
THE HALF-HEARTED
THE HOUSE OF THE FOUR WINDS
HUNTINGTOWER
THE ISLAND OF SHEEP
JOHN BURNET OF BARNS
THE LONG TRAVERSE
A LOST LADY OF OLD YEARS
MIDWINTER
THE PATH OF THE KING
THE POWER-HOUSE
PRESTER JOHN
A PRINCE OF THE CAPTIVITY
THE RUNAGATES CLUB
SALUTE TO ADVENTURERS
THE SCHOLAR GIPSIES
SICK HEART RIVER
THE THIRTY-NINE STEPS
THE THREE HOSTAGES
THE WATCHER BY THE THRESHOLD
WITCH WOOD

**NON-FICTION**

AUGUSTUS
THE CLEARING HOUSE
JULIUS CAESAR
THE KING'S GRACE
THE MASSACRE OF GLENCOE
MONTROSE
OLIVER CROMWELL
SIR WALTER RALEIGH
SIR WALTER SCOTT

# JOHN BUCHAN
## GORDON AT KHARTOUM

HOUSE OF
STRATUS

This edition published in 2008 by House of Stratus, an imprint of Stratus Books Ltd., 21 Beeching Park, Kelly Bray, Cornwall, PL17 8QS, UK.

www.houseofstratus.com

Typeset, printed and bound by House of Stratus.

A catalogue record for this book is available from the British Library.

ISBN 07511-170-0-X

MY DEAR EVELYN BARING,

I have heard part of the story which I have told in these pages from the lips of those who shared in it; from Kitchener, from Slatin, and especially from your father. As a young man I owed so much to Lord Cromer that I should like to inscribe this little book to his son.

J B

# CONTENTS

# PROLOGUE

In the first days of November in the year 1883 an observer on the palace roof at Khartoum would have been struck by an unwonted quiet. The great spaces around him were as they had always been – the blue waters of the two rivers sweeping to their junction, the green patches of dhurra and the fronded palm trees on their banks, the tracts of tawny grass and thorn and sand stretching to little ribs of hill, black in the noon sunshine and rose-red at twilight. But in the sprawling city of mud and brick at his feet there was an ominous stillness. There was some stir indeed at the new fortifications which were being constructed two miles to the south, but the troops there wrought languidly, for they were mostly old and crippled. The racial hotchpotch in the streets, Cairene officials, Coptic clerks, Greek and Arab traders, and Negroes of a hundred tribes, had been solemnised into a painful expectancy. Rumours came hourly, the wild tattle of the East, and all the rumours were bad. The new prophet of God, the Mahdi, was master of Kordofan. His lieutenant, Osman Digna, the slave-merchant of Suakim, had fired the eastern Soudan. The provincial governors, Slatin in Darfur, Lupton in the Bahr-el-Ghazal, Emin in Equatoria, were in deadly peril. An army of 10,000 men under Hicks Pasha, a British officer, had marched into the western desert to deal with the enemy – a ragged, ill-trained army, but the only thing that stood between Khartoum and ruin. The word, the too true word, that was being whispered in the bazaars was that that army had perished.

At the moment Egypt bore nominal rule over a domain extending from the Mediterranean to the Equator, and from the Sahara to the Red Sea. But in most of the country south of Wadi Halfa, which we know as the Soudan, the writ of the Khedive ran limpingly or not at all. The territory was larger than all western Europe, nearly a million square miles, and it was held by scattered Egyptian posts who at that time ranked as among the worst soldiers in the world.

Till the second decade of the nineteenth century the Soudan had had no history. The great empires of the ancient world had done no more than touch its fringes. It was a mystery land out of which came tales of snow mountains, and monstrous beasts and men, and fabulous treasures of gold. Broken tribes from Arabia crossed the Red Sea, intermingled with the Negro inhabitants, and spread the faith of Islam, but to Europe it was only a name till that 'barbarian of genius,' the Albanian tobacco-seller, Mohammed Ali, made it part of Egypt. Like Cambyses he sought an El Dorado in the south; he desired for the sake of Egyptian irrigation to secure the upper waters of the Nile; visions of Napoleonic conquests, too, surged in his fantastic brain. Khartoum ceased to be a collection of reed huts and became the capital of a new empire, and a mighty emporium of the slave trade. But the empire was miserably and corruptly governed, and instead of an asset it proved a millstone round Egypt's neck. Ismail, who came to the throne in 1873, was also in his own way a man of genius. He essayed reforms, but no patching could preserve a structure so ill-founded. He would have crushed the slave trade, but his officials battened on it. He would have introduced order and justice, but his mudirs and beys were incompetent and his soldiers ran away. In 1883 the government of the Soudan was a jerry-built monstrosity which would have fallen from its own weight even if there had been no alien force to batter it. Ismail was the typical Oriental despot whose imagination, especially in money matters, far outran the prosaic fact. But there was an element of greatness in his folly. When he was asked concerning the gauge of his proposed Soudan railway, he replied, 'Make it the same as South Africa; it will save trouble in the end.'

Misgovernment was universal and enormous. A plague of rapacious underlings covered the land. The slave trade, officially forbidden, was unofficially encouraged. There was little law at the centre, and only anarchy at the circumference. Small wonder that the name of Egyptian or 'Turk' stank in Soudanese nostrils. Efforts to sweep the chamber only meant that seven new devils arrived when the broom was withdrawn. But let it be admitted that in 1883 the task was not easy. Egypt had neither the money nor the quality of man for so great an undertaking. The vast distances and the inadequate transport made a tight hand difficult. The land was an ethnological museum, and there was no economic or racial unity among its people. The population of the shabby little towns and villages was as mongrel as that of a seaport in the Levant. North of the thirteenth parallel of latitude lived the tribes of camel-owning Arabs, such as the Kababish and the Hadendowa. South of it, where the rainfall was heavier and there were pastures and forests, dwelt the cattle-owning Arabs, including the great clan of the Baggara, and south again the Negroes of Equatoria. These last formed the hunting ground of the slave dealers, notably the Baggara, whom Sir Reginald Wingate has called the Red Indians of the Soudan. In such a racial medley there were only two elements of union. There was a universal hatred of the Cairo government; and, in the priest-ridden villages and among the nomads of the wilds, there was a smouldering fire of religious fanaticism, which might break forth with the suddenness and fury of a desert sandstorm.

The Soudan, as I have said, had no unity and no history, nothing to bind it together except the long silver thread of the Nile. In 1883 to the Western world it was still largely unknown, though Speke and Baker, Gordon and Stanley had interested

Europe in its southern fringes... Suddenly the fates set the play. From Darfur to the Red Sea, from Assouan to the Great Lakes, it became a single stage, lit by the fires of death, and as the months passed the drama drew to its climax in the few square miles of land where Khartoum stood at the junction of the two Niles. The ancient river of Egypt, which had witnessed in its lower course the making of so much history, now saw in its southern wilds a tragedy evolve itself with half the world as breathless spectators.

# DRAMATIS PERSONAE

It was no drama of blind, illogical happenings. The action was determined by the character of four men whom destiny brought into ironic conjunction. Let us glance at these in turn, beginning with the most distant and the most potent.

## I

Mr Gladstone in 1883 was in his seventy-fourth year. For the second time he was chief Minister of the Crown, and the year before he had celebrated his parliamentary jubilee. He had been returned to power in 1880 with a great majority, after a campaign of brilliant electioneering devices, in which, in spite of his age, he had played the major part. By millions of his countrymen he was passionately hated and distrusted, and by millions he was passionately adored. He had long ago formally discarded the Tory faith in which he had begun his career, but his mind remained tenaciously conservative, and the half-dozen Liberal principles which made up his professed creed were held with as blind a devotion as any Tory ever gave to Church and King. He had received, as he thought, a mandate from the nation for a programme of reconstruction at home and peace abroad – a widening of the franchise, a generous settlement of the Irish imbroglio, land reform, economy in expenditure, and, abroad, a recoil both from Palmerston's habit of light-hearted foreign adventure and from Disraeli's policy of imperial expansion. So far he had not been fortunate. Ireland was proving a thornier problem than he had thought; in South Africa he had had to face disaster and humiliation; and in Egypt he was confronted with a situation which promised much embarrassment and little profit.

'The difficulties of the case,' he told the House of Commons two years later, 'have passed entirely beyond the limits of such political and military difficulties as I have known in the course of an experience of half a century.' By that time some of the troubles were of his own making, but when he took office he inherited a quandary for which he was in no way to blame. The cutting of the Suez Canal had involved Britain irrevocably in Egypt's affairs, both as a shareholder in the Canal and as the guardian of the road to India. Mr Gladstone, anxious to have as little as possible to do with the Nile valley, had been compelled by the force of circumstances to armed intervention. Alexandria had been bombarded by British warships, and Arabi's rebellion had been crushed at Tel-el-Kebir by British troops. There was a force of British regulars in Egypt, and the Egyptian army and the Egyptian police were under British officers.

Lord Granville, his Foreign Secretary, had been dragged by Gambetta into the policy of the Joint Note, which made foreign intervention inevitable, but France had drawn back and left Britain to face the consequences. It was necessary to get the finances straight in the interest both of the foreign bondholders and the Egyptian people. It was necessary to liquidate many of the valueless territorial assets which Ismail had accumulated. No mere appointment of commissions to report would meet the need; nor could a public declaration of non-responsibility make Britain irresponsible. She was in military occupation of a country which the native rulers and the suzerain Turkey were alike incompetent to govern; and, since she had the power, the civilised world and her own conscience saddled her with the duty. But it was a duty which in the nature of things could be neither simple nor clear, for Egypt was a labyrinth of paradox. 'One alien race,' in Lord

Milner's words, 'had to control and guide a second alien race, the Turks, by whom they were disliked, in the government of a third race, the Egyptians.' And there was the eternal international paradox, that France laboured to put obstacles in the path of a British policy for which Britain was utterly disinclined, and by her efforts succeeded against her will in forcing an unwilling Britain to do what neither Power wanted.

Mr Gladstone was not altogether fortunate in his colleagues. Lord Morley has told us that 'no more capable set of ruling men were ever got together than the Cabinet of 1880.' Such can scarcely be the verdict of history. The Cabinet in 1882 was a mosaic of old Whigs and new Radicals. There was a Palmerstonian strain in it, and a restless experimental yeast, and a considerable spice of the bland and leisurely eighteenth-century tradition. It was not a body from which in a crisis the nation could look for a shrewd reading of facts, instant decision, and swift action. Only two members had that rare thing, political genius – Mr Chamberlain at the Board of Trade, who was immersed in departmental business, and the Prime Minister himself. The old man of seventy-four so towered above his colleagues in popular prestige, in parliamentary skill, and in moral force that when he bestirred himself his will was law.

As compared with the riches of his great rival Mr Gladstone's mind was equipped like a Victorian dining-room – a few heavy pieces of furniture and these not of the best pattern. He cannot interest his successors as Disraeli interests them, for he had nothing of the artist in him, and little of the philosopher. He was without the gift of style, and has left no spoken or written word by which the world can remember him. We cannot recapture the impression of his uncanny House of Commons dexterity, or his Sinaitic platform thunderings, or his wonderful presence – the grim lips, the great nose, and the flashing aquiline eye. He was a supreme master of a talent by which Britain was governed for two hundred years, but now the fashion has passed away, and that intricate and sonorous declamation is as remote from reality as church bells heard among the guns of war. The causes he fought for have been won and forgotten, or rejected and forgotten, and give small title to immortality.

But the man himself remains a marvel and a mystery – a character far subtler and more baffling than Disraeli's. Like some mediaeval ecclesiastic he professed the half-dozen dogmas of his faith as a rigid and infallible canon, but, like such an ecclesiastic, he showed supreme ingenuity in their interpretation. He had as high a courage as was ever possessed by an English statesman; no man cultivated the masses more assiduously – or feared them less. He was not inaccessible to the teaching of facts, but his nature was such that he would ignore facts unless he could subsume them under one of his fixed categories of thought. The self-deception of which he has been accused was the effort of a mind fundamentally rigid to keep its orthodoxy inviolate, and yet continue to guide affairs and to master men. He convinced himself that he longed for retirement, but the powers which nature had given him of dominating his followers could not be laid down till the grave.

He was as sensitive as Disraeli on the question of national prestige, and would tolerate no incivility from Bismarck or anybody else. It made him furious to think that any foreign Government should have the notion of him that the Emperor Nicholas had of Lord Aberdeen. As a man of deep religious convictions and high and humane instincts he was sensitive, too, about the honour and morality of any course. But in a sudden crisis in foreign affairs he might be a dangerous leader. In the first place he was slow to realise a situation, having a short-range imagination and little power of visualising unfamiliar things. Again, his habit of mind made it a laborious task for him to admit concessions or changes into a policy which he had once accepted, the more if such changes infringed ever so slightly one of the cast-iron articles of his creed. Again, the leisurely administrative ritual in which he had been trained made him averse to any swift action; emergencies he held to be a word which should be omitted from a statesman's vocabulary, since it was his business to see that they did not arise. Above all, his enormous self-confidence inclined him to defy the clamour of fact as he would have defied the clamour of a mob... Such a one might well be a protagonist in an Aristotelian tragedy, if circumstances arose which made certain elements in his strength a deadly weakness.

## II

In September 1883 Sir Evelyn Baring arrived in Egypt. He was then a man of forty-two who had had much varied experience since he began life in the Royal Artillery. His earliest connection with the Nile valley was in 1846, when as a child he watched Ibrahim Pasha driving in St James's Park. Under Disraeli's Government he had been one of the Commissioners of the Egyptian debt, and in 1879 had resigned the post in despair. On Ismail's fall he returned to Egypt as Controller of the Debt, and after a year went to India as Financial Member of Council. In 1883, when Sir Edward Malet was promoted to the Embassy at Brussels, he returned to Cairo as his successor.

The maker of modern Egypt began his career there as British Resident, a post anomalous and undefined; the authority of the office was only such as its occupier could make it. Baring was unknown to the British public, but he had a considerable reputation among men associated with imperial affairs, and he had some prestige with Mr Gladstone's Government. In politics he was a Liberal; he was a friend of the Prime Minister; his cousin Lord Northbrook was in the Cabinet. His proved competence in financial questions seemed to mark him out as the man to handle a problem which was believed to be mainly financial. He had no melodramatic imperial dreams, and would gladly have seen Britain rid of Egypt altogether, believing that we needed it no more than, to quote Lord Palmerston, a man with an estate in the north of England and a residence in the south needed the possession of the inns on the North Road. But he recognised that Britain had assumed responsibilities which she could not relinquish, and from

India he had observed with some bewilderment Mr Gladstone's behaviour about Alexandria – his refusal to allow the landing of any force to protect life and property on the ground that such an act would constitute an 'assumption of authority,' while he considered that the bombardment of the Egyptian forts was not such an assumption. He embarked upon his Egyptian duties with an uneasy feeling that he might find Downing Street a little difficult.

But in one matter he was wholly in accord with his superiors. He saw before him a gigantic task: the rescue of a land from insolvency and a people from beggary, overdue schemes of public works, legal, educational and administrative reform, and a perpetual diplomatic strife with obstructive Powers. Egypt must begin by cutting her losses and getting rid of the Soudan. His view was that of Lord Granville. 'It takes away somewhat of the position of a man to sell his racers and hunters, but if he cannot afford to keep them, the sooner they go to Tattersall's the better.'

The quality of the future Lord Cromer was in 1883 not revealed to the world, but the man was already formed, and the hour for him had come. In his leisure he had made himself an excellent scholar; he was widely and deeply read and full of the spirit of old good books, so he had a philosophy of conduct behind him. But he was above all a practical man, with a keen eye to discern and a just mind to weigh the facts of a case. In all heart-breaking tangles there is usually one problem which is the key of the whole. The ordinary man fusses about among a multitude, tinkers a little here and a little there, finds nothing come of it, and gives up the business in disgust. The wise man seizes upon the one thing needful, and discovers when he has achieved this that all things are added unto him. Baring saw that the key of Egypt was finance, that everything depended upon financial solvency, and that his first duty was to nurse her assets. In this task he had only the official status which he could create for himself. To many at first he seemed brusque and imperious. Gordon, when he met him, thought him 'pretentious, grand, patronizing.' He certainly did not suffer fools gladly, and he had a detestation of all tall talk and bravado and advertisement. But in his own way he was an incomparable diplomatist, for he diffused an atmosphere of goodwill and utter sincerity. His brusqueness was not due to restless nerves, for he had the patience of a sculptured king on a monument. His motto was that sentence from Bacon which he often quoted: 'It were good that men in their Innovations should follow the example of Time itself, which, indeed, innovateth greatly, but quietly, and by degrees scarce to be perceived.' In action he showed a wise parsimony, the courage to do nothing when action was futile, to go slowly when a thousand hysterical critics urged him to speed.

In all this there was some surface resemblance to Mr Gladstone's own creed, the dislike of adventure, the insistence upon prosaic economic truths, even to Lord Granville's urbane impassivity. But the difference was profound. Baring was incapable of dawdling. His caution was the consequence of a true reading of the case, not of setting it aside. His patience was a reasoned policy, and not due to a vacant brain or a halting will. When the time came no man could strike more swiftly or more surely. Above all he had a mind wholly honest with itself. He did not believe that an ugly fact could be got rid of by pretending that it was not there, or that a plain moral duty could be ingeniously explained away.

## III

In the early 'forties there was born in Dongola a certain Mohammed Ahmed, the son of a priest who belonged to a noted family of boatbuilders. His father died while he was young, and he grew up with his uncle and brothers on the wooded island of Abba, in the White Nile above Khartoum. Very early he discovered a vocation for the religious life, but he could find no place for himself in the local hierarchy. He saw the practice of his faith clogged with impurities, he saw the children of Islam ground under the heel of foreign oppressors who in the name of the

Prophet betrayed the Prophet's cause, so he retired into solitude to wait for a revelation. For some years in a cave on the island he lived the life of a hermit. He was a most impressive young man, of great physical beauty, with a voice which thrilled his hearers, and with a power of oratory which turned their heads. He preached a doctrine of poverty and abstinence, and something more – a restoration of Islam to its primitive purity and of his countrymen to power and freedom. The fame of the recluse at Abba spread far and wide through the Soudan, and his mystical prophecies were whispered from mouth to mouth. Legends grew of his miracle-working, and of his visions when the Prophet communed with him in the night watches. People journeyed from great distances to sit at his feet, among them an obscure man of the Baggara, one Abdullah, who was not interested in mysticism, but who was determined to rid his land of foreigners and rule in their stead. The young prophet was known as Zahed, the Renouncer, but there were already many who called him the Redeemer.

In 1881 the moment arrived for his epiphany. He cunningly knit up various legends of the Mohammedan world into one. The Twelfth Imam had been long hidden from men: he was the Twelfth Imam. A Messiah had been promised, a Mahdi or 'guide,' who would convert the whole world to the faith of Islam: he was that Mahdi. In May he sent round a proclamation to the neighbouring tribes announcing his advent, and his mission to purify and lead to victory all true believers and to regenerate the land. He had many things in his favour. He claimed to be of the blood of the Prophet. His age was forty, the traditional age for a Messiah. He had the mole on the cheek and the V-shaped gap between his front teeth which were looked on as proof of a high destiny. Above all he had his name for saintliness and austerity, his magnetic personality, his winning eloquence, his repute for miraculous powers and for converse with the unseen. In all likelihood he was wholly sincere in his claims, for years of seclusion and introverted thought may well pervert a man's vision.

The

MAP OF THE SOUDAN

Egyptian authorities at Khartoum had hitherto respected the saint, but they were bound to take order with the rebel. They stumbled from blunder to blunder. In August an attempt was made to arrest him, and the police force sent for the purpose was ignominiously beaten off by men armed only with clubs. The story of the victory flew through the Soudan. Mohammed Ahmed, realising that he had burned his boats, followed the example of the Prophet and made a *Hejira* into the mountains of southern Kordofan and the country of the Baggara. There he proclaimed a *Jehad*, a holy war to free the Soudan, conquer Egypt, take Constantinople, and convert the world. Like the Prophet he appointed four caliphs, of whom the chief was the fierce Abdullah. Men flocked to his standard, slave raiders who had chafed at Gordon's restraint, wandering tribes of the desert who saw a chance of war and plunder, all who had suffered injustice from the tax-gatherer and the kourbash. Soon he had an army of thousands, called 'dervishes,' which means poor men, wearing the patched cotton smock or jibbah, which was the mark of poverty. Abdullah and his brother caliphs presently organised them into some semblance of an army. The governor of Fashoda sent an expedition against them, and the expedition did not return. Some months later Khartoum sent 3000 men, and they too were utterly destroyed. With three victories behind him the Mahdi in the summer of 1882 descended from the mountains and entered upon his career of conquest.

The capital of Kordofan, El Obeid, to begin with, made a stout resistance, and in the first action the Mahdi lost 10,000 men. But the flame of fanaticism was only kindled to greater fury by the check, and the straw tents of the besiegers crept like a locust drift around the city. In January 1883, El Obeid capitulated. Egypt made one last crazy effort at reconquest. Troops were hurried to Khartoum, and Hicks Pasha was despatched in September with 10,000 men, to crush the rebels and relieve Slatin in Darfur. On November 3, in a forest near El Obeid, he met an Arab army 40,000 strong, and few of his command survived to tell the tale. The Mahdi celebrated his victory with a salute of many guns. Before the end of the year Slatin had surrendered Darfur, and Osman Digna was mopping up the garrisons in the eastern Soudan. South of Berber only the Khartoum area and a few isolated posts were outside the rule of the new Messiah.

The man who had wrought these miracles was no mere charlatan. He had put life into a dead people, and turned beasts of burden into warriors, and such a feat is beyond the common impostor. He had a quick sense of the theatrical and knew how to stage his appearances so as to impress his followers; but, though he might put pepper in his fingernails to expedite the flow of tears and paint his eyes to enhance their lustre, he believed in his mission as fervently as any Christian saint. He organised his following on a basis of extreme puritanism – the simplest food and dress, shaven heads, the prohibition of wine and tobacco, oaths and gaming and dancing – and any offence, however slight, was savagely punished. Had he been also a military genius, he might have built up a new and most formidable type of army. As it was he created a fighting brotherhood, sustained by religious ardour and a long tale of past wrongs. Like many prophets he did not practise what he preached, for in the seclusion of their inner tents he and his caliphs wallowed in debaucheries. But when he showed himself in public, to the wild Baggara and the credulous Soudanese he must have seemed indeed the chosen of Heaven. Not for centuries had the faith of Islam, 'There is but the one God and Mohammed is his prophet' – the eternal truth and the necessary lie – been preached by such compelling lips. He was tall and strongly built, with a carefully trimmed black beard; his colour was the light brown of the Dongolawi; he had a noble head, well-cut features, a mouth that was always smiling, dark eyes that both wooed and commanded, and an exquisite voice. His jibbah, as became a Messiah, was not dirty and patched, but speckless, and he exhaled a delicious perfume. Men said it was the odour of Paradise, and that it was natural that it should attend him, for was he not always communing with God and the Prophet and the great Angels?

## IV

In the autumn of 1883 a certain major-general in the British Army was coming to the end of a leisurely tour of Palestine. He had been studying the sites of famous Scriptural places, notably Golgotha and the Temple of Jerusalem, staying with missionaries and with the eccentric Laurence Oliphant at Mount Carmel, varying his reflections on religion with schemes for letting the Mediterranean into the cleft of the Jordan valley and so making a new canal to the Red Sea. This soldier, Charles George Gordon, was now fifty years of age, but his spare figure and scarcely grizzled hair suggested a younger man. He was about the middle height, with a slight stoop, as if he were looking for something just beyond his reach. Everything about him, his light step, his quick impetuous speech, spoke of intense vitality. He smiled much, but his face in repose was stern and rather melancholy. Tropic suns had not spoiled the freshness of his skin. The forehead was broad, and he had the high cheekbones of his Scottish ancestry; the jaw was strong, and the mouth under the small moustache was firm and a little grim. But the arresting feature was the eyes. They were of a brilliant blue, set far apart, restless, ardent, capable of melting into an infinite kindliness but also of blazing into a formidable wrath. His whole *régard* suggested simplicity and modesty, but also an extreme tenacity of purpose. It was the face of an adventurer in the worlds of both flesh and spirit.

He was a lonely being, whose mind was always turning inward. In his own profession he had a multitude of acquaintances, but few friends. His intimates, with whom he constantly corresponded, were certain parsons at home and his elder sister Augusta. He was shabbily dressed, and seemed to desire above all things to escape notice and to be left in peace with his thoughts. Yet this man had behind him a career which for varied and desperate enterprise had no parallel in the world at that day. More than once he had been in the glare of publicity, and his name was somewhere at the back of people's memories, much like that of Colonel T E Lawrence in our own day after his Arabian exploits were ended.

Gordon was born of one of those peripatetic soldier families which have long lost any territorial link with home. He entered the Royal Engineers, and in his early twenties went through the Crimean War with distinction, making there two lifelong friends, Garnet Wolseley and Gerald Graham. At twenty-seven he went to China, and at thirty found himself in command of a Chinese army. The tale of his doings in the Far East is in itself an epic, which cannot be told here. Suffice it to say that by his courage and military capacity he suppressed a dangerous rebellion, won the admiration and confidence of so formidable a figure as Li Hung Chang, was made a Mandarin and a Field-Marshal, and was offered and refused vast wealth and many honours. Another man might have used his power to win a kingdom and to found a dynasty, but Gordon's thoughts were not on such things. He returned home with a prodigious reputation, for he was 'Chinese Gordon' to the English people, but this young man of thirty-two declined to be lionised and shunned the mention of his exploits as if they had been a disgrace. He was content to settle down to prosaic regimental duties at Gravesend, where he filled his leisure with good works, especially the care of poor boys, and with preaching quietly his religious faith. He lived bare, spending most of his small income in charity, and he sent the gold medal which the Emperor of China had given him to be sold for the relief of the Lancashire cotton famine. But he was always a keen professional soldier, and he was still worldly enough to pine for more active service. The chance came when he met Nubar Pasha at Constantinople in 1872 and was offered the governorship of the Khedive's Equatorial province in succession to Sir Samuel Baker. On January 28, 1874, he left home to take up the post. It was his forty-first birthday, and the day when the news of the death of David Livingstone came to England.

Equatoria was the second epic tale in Gordon's life. He had two main purposes; to suppress the slave trade, and, as a means to this end, to open up communication with the Great Lakes and once for all to dispel their mystery. He served Ismail with the same single-hearted zeal with which he had served the Chinese Emperor. He had able lieutenants, among them that great gentleman, the Italian Romolo Gessi, but he himself with his hard body, tireless energy, and unfaltering courage was the inspiration of every enterprise and the executant of most. It was a thankless labour to make a civilised state out of the squalid little towns and the immense trackless hinterland, and to enforce law and order with penny-steamers and fever-ridden soldiers 'as brave as hares.' But he never faltered and rarely despaired. He dreamed of a great Central African state where the well-being of the natives would be the Government's first care, a state extending through the present Kenya to the sea, and he conceived that he might be the man destined by God to redeem Egypt, that famous Bible land. He wrote in his journal:

> Comfort-of-Body – a very strong gentleman – says, 'You are well; you have done enough; go home; go home and be quiet and risk no more.' Mr Reason says, 'What is the use of opening more country to such a Government? There is more now under their power than they will ever manage.' …But then Something (I do not know what) says, 'Shut your eyes to what may happen in the future; leave that to God, and do what you think will open the country to both lakes. Do this, not for H H, or for his Government, but do it blindly and in faith.'

Such are the doubts which must always attend a crusader.

Equatoria was mainly a business of administration and exploration. The third epic tale in Gordon's life moved to a brisker tune. In 1877 Ismail made him Governor-General of the whole Soudan from the Tropic of Cancer to the Equator. Now began those marvellous camel-rides when Gordon sped like a flame across the deserts and surprised his enemies while they were still conspiring. He dismissed incompetents wholesale, and built up some semblance of a civil service and an army. He clipped the wings of Zobeir, the great slave dealer of the Bahr-el-Ghazal. On one occasion he covered on his camel eighty-five miles in thirty-six hours and rode alone into the enemy's camp, paralysing their hostility by his naked courage. But meantime the affairs of Egypt were hastening to perdition, and he was summoned to Cairo to discuss financial problems which he did not understand. He liked Ismail and thought that he was hardly treated by the Powers; he regarded the bondholders as common usurers: his health was beginning to crack and he believed that he had *angina pectoris*; in any case his work in the Soudan was at an end if Egypt had to think twice about every piastre. He accepted a last mission to the lunatic King John of Abyssinia, a potentate who was drunk every night and up at dawn every morning reading the Psalms. Early in 1880 he was back in England.

Then followed two years of odd jobs. Gordon had returned with a great repute among all those interested in African problems, but, as after China, his one desire seemed to be to bury himself. He rejoiced at Mr Gladstone's victory at the polls, and accepted the post of private secretary to Lord Ripon, the new Viceroy of India. Within a week he resigned. He went to Peking, where his influence prevented a war with Russia. Then he went on regimental duty to Mauritius, to oblige a brother officer, and spent some peaceful months in that island in religious meditation. 'God has been very merciful to me,' he wrote, 'in the thoughts I have had here (in Patmos) regarding the Scriptures and the motives of one's actions: and now, through His mercy, I see lakes and seas of knowledge before me.' After that he was summoned to South Africa, where he gave his mind to the native question, but found it impossible to work with the Cape Government. In January 1883 he was in Jerusalem, taking a holiday at last, and feeling himself a hopeless misfit. Africa had laid its spell upon him, and meditations as to the exact measurements of Solomon's Temple could not oust his interest in the Nile valley, of which the northern part seemed to be now in chaos and the centre in flames. The King of the Belgians was making overtures to him, and he was seriously thinking of going to the Congo. He still felt within him the conviction that he was born to rule men and that war was his true province, and he had reasons for his belief. In China he had shown the talents of a commander-in-chief, and in the Soudan those of an incomparable cavalry leader. He had the gifts of foresight, judgment, swift decision, and lightning execution. His old comrade Wolseley was now the soldier best spoken of in Britain, but Gordon for all his modesty knew that he had powers in him to which Wolseley could make no claim.

Let us look more closely at the character of this man, now waiting at Jaffa for a cable from King Leopold, and about to enter upon the fourth and greatest epic of his life. He had a mind which was a strange blend of crudity and power. He had little knowledge of the world outside his profession; his education had been slight and was not supplemented by later study except constant reading of the Bible: his views on ordinary questions, economic, educational and political, were often shrewd but were not based on any considered philosophy of life, and the cosmogony in which he believed was mediaeval in its simplicity. He had a quick eye for facts, and his judgment on matters with which he was acquainted was mostly sound and penetrating, but on other subjects few men could talk wilder nonsense. Like Cromwell, he relied more on instinct than on reason; his first summing up of a situation, his first impression of a man, was commonly his last.

His heart was tender, and he hated all cruelty and injustice. 'I am averse to the loss of a single life,' he was always declaring. But his temper was often out of control, and he was capable of great harshness. His humility before his Maker did not make him humble before his fellow-mortals, and he bore himself to British and Egyptian grandees with a pride which in another would have been arrogance. The result was a good deal of friction. 'What a queer life mine has been,' he wrote to his sister, 'with these fearful rows continually occurring.' He was not an easy man to work with, for he had moods of extreme irritability and petulance, which he sincerely repented. ' Talk of two natures in one,' he said. 'I have a hundred, and they none think alike and all want to rule.' With a deep love and charity towards mankind, he could be grossly uncharitable in his behaviour to individuals, and men whose affections he had won by his gentleness would be amazed when his eyes 'like blue diamonds' blazed at some trifle with wrath or hardened into a stony hostility. To Cuzzi and Slatin he was relentless even in his own extremity, for they had committed the unforgivable sin of denying their Lord. In that he was a crusader, but he could also be the knight errant, and he would have challenged Nubar to a duel because the Egyptian had insulted a fellow Companion of the Bath. His instincts were not harmonised and were often at war. His habits were temperate, indeed ascetic, for he had trained his body to need little nourishment and little sleep, but now and then he had unregenerate longings for home when he could have oysters to lunch and not get up till noon. He made sparing use of wine and spirits, but he smoked incessantly, though he tried often to give up tobacco, reminding himself that his body was the temple of the Holy Spirit. The smug gentility of Victorian England he had at all times detested, and he carried his dislike so far as to be scornful even of ordinary etiquette, perhaps because he knew that in his inmost heart he had a liking for ceremonial. When the Prince of Wales asked him to dinner, he declined on the ground that he always went to bed at nine o'clock.

Gordon was so unlike other men, so apparently single-hearted, and radiating such an atmosphere of moral fervour, that he readily acquired a spiritual ascendancy over all who knew him well and many who did not. Wolseley, who did not lack self-confidence, felt that he was 'not worthy to pipe-clay his belt.' But the dualism which was notable in his lesser qualities was also in the very foundation of his being. The impression of single-heartedness was an illusion, for all his life his soul was the stage of a conflict.

Like Lee and Stonewall Jackson and many another great soldier, he had that scorn of death which comes from an abiding sense of the littleness of life. Man's efforts seemed to him only a child's game played out under the calm eyes of God. He had moments of self-abasement. 'If a man speaks well of me, divide it by millions and then it will be millions of times too favourable. If a man speaks evil of me, multiply it by millions and it will be millions of times too favourable.' The world of sense shrank to a pin-head when he contemplated the eternity beyond the grave. The rush of Time's winged chariot was never out of his ears. The irony of human life was always present to him, the fragility of its hopes, the comedy of its trivial ambitions. 'It matters little,' he wrote to Lord Lyons. 'A few years hence a piece of ground six feet by three will contain all that remains of Ambassadors, Ministers, and your obedient humble servant C G Gordon.' And in a robuster mood he could even laugh at it all.

> In ten or twelve years' time, Baring, Lord Wolseley, myself, Evelyn Wood, will have no teeth and will be deaf; some of us will be quite *passé*; no one will come and court us. New Barings, new Lord Wolseleys will have arisen, who will call us 'bloaks' or 'twaddlers.' 'Oh! for goodness' sake, come away, man! Is that dreadful bore coming? If once he gets alongside you, you are in for half an hour,' will be the remark of some young captain of the present time on seeing you enter the Club. That is very humiliating, for we, each one, think we are immortal.

Such a habit of thought should have made its possessor a mystic and a recluse. But it was constantly jostled by another; in Raleigh's famous image, if one gate of his soul was open to 'divine contemplations,' the other was thronged by 'manifold vanities.' Conscious of great powers, he burned to use them, not for the sake of gauds and titles, but for the delight of their exercise. He longed for the joy of battle even when he knew the ultimate triviality of the issue. All his life this combat lasted. He fought against it; he choked down his passionate desire to explore the Great Lakes; he withdrew himself to Gravesend, to Mauritius, to Palestine, but the craving would not be stilled. The convictions of the quietist could not bridle the instincts of the born man of action. These extended even beyond the grave. 'Look on me now,' he once told a friend, 'with small armies to command and no cities to govern. I hope that death will set me free from pain, and that great armies will be given me, and that I shall have vast cities to govern.' This dual nature was both his strength and his weakness. It delivered him from fear and from all vulgar ambition, but it made him uncommonly difficult for prosaic folk to work with or to understand.

The religion, which was the mainstay of his life, was evangelical Christianity, coloured by a singular mind and temperament. It was based wholly on his reading of the Scriptures, and for orthodoxy in the common sense he cared not at all. He got little aid from the churches though much from individual ministers; he only discovered the value of the sacrament of communion late in his life, when he resolved to take what he called the 'eating' once a month. Many of his theological speculations were fantastic and some were heterodox. He was curiously tolerant of other creeds, and, unlike Doughty, had a respect for the fierce Moslem monotheism, regretting only that it was blind to the fact of Christ. In his social work, too, he indulged in no diatribes against the rich; he pitied them as much as he pitied the poor, and, like Christ, called them not knaves but fools. He accepted in the simplest sense every word of the Bible as a direct revelation, and was satisfied with even the rudimentary interpretation of the popular tract – at Gravesend he was a great tract distributor. The Apocalypse was his special delight, and he looked forward to the literal accomplishment of its tremendous prophecies, the Last Trump, Christ throned in the skies among flaming myriads, and the New Jerusalem descending visibly out of Heaven. He had decided that the Mount of Olives would be the scene of the Second Coming.

The two cornerstones of his faith were the divine ordering of every detail of the universe, and his union with God in Christ. His belief in predestination was no blind fatalism, for, though he knew that his life was in God's hands, he omitted no precaution to ensure the success of his work and his own health and safety. It was his duty to keep his powder dry. But, his task in that respect being done, the rest was in higher hands. In Equatoria he wrote:

> The intense comfort of no fear, no uneasiness about being ill, is very great, and more than half the cause of good health. No comfort is equal to that which he has who has God for his stay; who believes, not in words but in fact, that all things are ordained to happen and must happen. He who has this has already died, and is free from the annoyances of this life. I do not say I have attained to this perfect state, but I have it as my great desire.

And again:

> I am a chisel which cuts the wood; the Carpenter directs it. If I lose my edge, He must sharpen me; if He puts me aside, and takes another, it is His own good will. None are indispensable to Him; He will do His work with a straw equally as well.

And during his wild rides in the Soudan:

> My sense of independence is gone. I own nothing and am nothing. I am a pauper and seem to have ceased to exist. A sack of rice jolting along on a camel would do as much as I *think* I do.

This conviction of all things divinely ordained abased him before his Maker, but gave him a contemptuous condescension towards the common perils of life and the rivalries and ambitions of his fellow mortals. It was united with a passionate desire for communion with the unseen, for a closer walk with God, ever since at Gravesend a text from the Bible had flashed upon his brain and he had found in nearness to God the key of life. He trod the familiar path of the mystic. It was an unbroken communion, for he had none of Cromwell's agonies of estrangement, those tortures which are the fate of subtler and profounder spirits. His religion was more like that of Major-General Thomas Harrison, who walked confidently through life, looking forward happily to the command of the left wing at Armageddon. The one cloud came from his moods of insurgent ambition, when he longed to force the pace instead of waiting upon the divine call. To learn to wait in patience was the chief discipline of his life. This mystic, when he betook himself to pure contemplation, found something lacking; he was happiest when he was busiest, and when prayer was his refreshment and not the sole occupation of his day. He prayed at all times, for in prayer he felt himself at one with God, and through prayer he could benefit the world. He had a copy-book filled with the names of people for whom he prayed daily. The devout Mohammedans around him saw in this infidel one whose trust in Allah was stronger than their own, and his fame as a holy man soon equalled his repute as a warrior. To plain folk all the world over, the soldier-saint, the practical mystic, the iron dreamer is the leader whom in their hearts they desire.

So in the year 1883 four men from the ends of the earth were being drawn together to a clash of wills and purposes on a single stage. Three were in different ways men of an austere religion. All four had the tenacity of character and elevation of spirit which make the true tragic hero.

# ACT THE FIRST: THE MISSION

## I

In 1877 in a magazine article Mr Gladstone had written prescient words: 'Territorial questions are not to be disposed of by arbitrary limits... Our first site in Egypt, be it by larceny or by emption, will be the almost certain egg of a North African empire.' The arguments against British interference were unanswerable to a statesman whose mind was set upon home reform and who detested all grandiose foreign adventure. It would involve us in interminable diplomatic wrangles: it would vastly extend our military commitments, and in case of war it would dangerously enlarge our line of defence. Yet the logic of events had now made his discretion impossible. We had drifted into interference by steps which seemed inevitable in the retrospect. We had bombarded Alexandria and suppressed Arabi. British officers had been compelled to take in hand the reorganisation of the Egyptian army. There was a large force of British regulars in the country. The finances were under British control. The new Khedive's precarious throne was supported by British bayonets, and he had come to lean wholly on British advice. The suzerain Turkey would not, or could not, act as a protector. If Britain marched out another Power would march in, and the road to India would be in jeopardy. Besides, every consideration of public morals forbade us lightly to cast off responsibilities which we had ourselves created.

The position of supreme adviser demands that the advice given shall be continuous and shall cover the whole field of policy. It was obvious that the most difficult question was the future of the Soudan, but in this matter the British Government at first stubbornly refused to interest itself. In November 1882 Mr Gladstone had declared that it was no part of Britain's duty to restore order there. 'It is politically connected with Egypt in consequence of its very recent conquest; but it has not been included within the sphere of our operations, and we are by no means disposed to admit without qualification that it is within the sphere of our responsibility.' The view had sound reason in it, but its logical consequence was the abandonment of the Soudan at the earliest possible moment, and the discouragement of Egypt from any attempt at reconquest. But, though this abandonment was urged by Dufferin and Malet, the British Government declined to give any advice in the matter or to prohibit Hicks' ill-fated expedition.

It is important to distinguish between the knowledge which they possessed at the time and that which they afterwards acquired. They did not then realise – no one realised – the strength of the Mahdi's power. They were not fully aware of the feebleness of the Egyptian soldiery. But, nevertheless, it is impossible to acquit them of being false in substance to their own policy. Their duty was, in Britain's interest, to make Egypt face the facts which their own representatives were pressing on them. In words which Lord Cromer wrote at a later date, they 'took shelter behind an illusory abrogation of responsibility, which was a mere phantom of the diplomatic and parliamentary mind.' Lord Granville's supineness in the autumn of 1883 was the seed of all the future misfortunes.

Before the Hicks tragedy was known Baring had endeavoured to get Britain to commit herself on the relinquishment of the Soudan, and Lord Granville had replied that, if consulted, he should recommend evacuation within certain limits. Then came the terrible news from Kordofan, to be followed by tidings of further disasters in the Suakim neighbourhood. Egypt must be advised, for she was helpless. On December 10 Baring telegraphed that he must have definite instructions, and on the 12th that the Khedive placed himself unreservedly in the hands of Britain. The British Government were in difficulties that month, for there were acute dissensions in the Cabinet on the proposed Franchise bill, and on the Egyptian question they felt that, in Lord Salisbury's words, they were 'at the mercy of any fortuitous concurrence of fanaticisms or fads.'

But the decision could not be delayed. On December 13 Lord Granville telegraphed recommending the Khedive's ministers to 'come to an early decision to abandon all territory south of Assouan or at least of Wadi Halfa.' On January 1, 1884, Baring told his Government that he was getting daily proof that the execution of their policy, although I believe it to be the best of which the circumstances permit, will be a work of the greatest difficulty,' and added: 'If a policy of abandonment is carried out, Her Majesty's Government should certainly be prepared to exercise a far more direct interference in the Government of Egypt than had hitherto been contemplated.' On January 4 came the final declaration of the British view. The whole Soudan, including Khartoum and the Red Sea littoral, must be abandoned. 'It is essential,' Baring was told, 'that in important communications affecting Egypt the advice of Her Majesty's Government should be followed, as long as the provisional occupation continues. Ministers and Governors must carry out this advice or forfeit their offices.' The Egyptian Cabinet promptly resigned, and their successors were virtually British nominees. Britain, with extreme unwillingness and in considerable confusion of mind, had taken over the administration of the Nile valley. In Mr Gladstone's words, they were an Egyptian Government.

## II

In Baring's telegram of December 22 there had been a significant sentence: 'It would also be necessary to send an English officer to Khartoum, with full powers to withdraw all the garrisons in the Soudan and to make the best arrangements possible for the future government of the country.' Britain had refused to despatch troops against the Mahdi to check his career of conquest, but, having put herself in Egypt's place, she was bound in common decency to extricate the Egyptian garrisons and civil population, and also to provide for some semblance of order when they had gone. So Baring thought, and he was no Quixote. The second duty was perhaps less imperative, for its possibility of accomplishment was dim, but there was no question about the first.

The Government not unnaturally desired to meet their obligations as cheaply as possible. The use of a military force might land them in a campaign; therefore a civilian must be found who had the requisite knowledge and prestige. As anxious Ministers revolved the matter in their minds they remembered the strange man, who for twenty years had been flashing in and out of the public gaze. Three years before a high official had told Lord Salisbury: 'I should never recommend your lordship to send Gordon on a delicate diplomatic mission to Paris or Vienna or Berlin, but if you want some out-of-the-way piece of work to be done in an unknown and barbarous country, Gordon would be your man.' The saying had been repeated and remembered in governing circles. Dufferin, in his despatch from Egypt about the Soudan, had suggested that Gordon might undertake its administration 'without drawing upon Egypt either for men or money.' The notion finally penetrated the languid mind of Lord Granville, who was being slowly coerced into some kind of active policy. Soldiers like Sir Andrew Clarke were pressing the same proposal. Here was a chance of getting inexpensively out of an awkward situation. The Foreign Secretary wrote to Mr Gladstone asking if he had any objection to the use of Gordon, though he had 'a small bee in his bonnet.' The Prime Minister had none, so Baring was consulted.

At first Baring was unsympathetic. He had met Gordon when the latter had visited Cairo as Governor-General of the Soudan, and had not been impressed by his wisdom. He replied that the Egyptian Government thought it dangerous to appoint a Christian to a land which was in the throes of a religious movement. He seems to have still hoped that Egypt herself might manage the evacuation of the 21,000 troops and 11,000 civilians. But the report of Abd-el-Kader Pasha on the matter convinced him that the task was beyond the power of any Egyptian, and, after refusing Gordon a second time, he was compelled on January 16 to send a telegram accepting him on certain conditions.

Meantime the situation had changed at home. Gordon to the man in the street had suddenly become a magical name. Sir Samuel Baker had written to *The Times* pressing for his appointment with all the weight of his great experience. In the popular press what is called in modern jargon a 'stunt' was in progress. Mr W T Stead, who in the *Pall Mall Gazette* appealed to both the serious and the excitable, had an interview with Gordon in his sister's house in Southampton, and came away with a copy of the *Imitation of Christ* and a sensational story which he made the most of in his paper. In Gordon's view, as Mr Stead reported it, Britain must either surrender everything to the Mahdi or at all hazards defend Khartoum. His reputation had always been high in evangelical circles, but now it grew to legendary heights, not only among the devout and among those who were scrupulous for British honour, but also among the classes who were already spoken of as Jingoes. 'Chinese Gordon for the Soudan!' became a national slogan. Gordon must be sent and no other. It was a demand for a man and not for a policy, for very few had any notion what the policy should be.

Mr Gladstone, we may believe in the light of after events, was little moved by the popular clamour. He was at Hawarden when Lord Granville telegraphed suggesting that Gordon should be sent to Suakim, to use his influence over the tribes to help in the evacuation to that port of the Khartoum population which Abd-el-Kader Pasha was believed to be organising. The Prime Minister offered no objection. This was on January 14. Next day Gordon saw Wolseley at the War Office and made a note of his proposed duties, the chief point of which was that he should go to Suakim, report on the military situation, and then return – a mere mission of inquiry. It was this scheme which Mr Gladstone finally accepted – one differing from Lord Granville's former plan, since it was advisory only instead of being partly executive, and it was this which was pressed on Baring. The Prime Minister was in a mood of extreme caution. He respected Gordon as a good Christian, but he had heard disquieting rumours of his difficulty as a subordinate. 'While his opinion on the Soudan,' he warned Lord Granville, 'may be of great value, we must be very careful in any instructions we give, that he does not shift the centre of gravity as to political and military responsibility for that country. In brief, if he reports what should be done, he should not be a judge *who* should do it, nor ought he to commit us on that point by advice officially given. It would be extremely difficult after sending him to reject such advice, and it should, therefore, I think, be made clear that he is not an agent for the purpose of advising on that point.' Now Lord Granville's telegram to Baring offering Gordon crossed one from Baring asking for 'a qualified British officer to go to Khartoum *with full powers civil and military to conduct the retreat*.' Lord Granville had offered an adviser and Baring asked for an executant. When later in the day the latter accepted Gordon, he accepted him in the sense of his own telegram. The game of cross-purposes had begun.

Gordon after seeing Wolseley had gone to Brussels. He was recalled on the 17th by telegram, and reached London early on the morning of the 18th. He went to the War Office, where he saw the Secretary of State, Lord Hartington, and the only other Cabinet Ministers who were in town, Lord Granville, Lord Northbrook and Sir Charles Dilke. It is clear that this truncated

Cabinet, having received Baring's last telegram, had on their own account gone well beyond the proposal which the Prime Minister had authorised. There was no talk now of a purely advisory mission. Gordon was not to report on evacuation but to carry it out. That at any rate was plain to his own mind, as is borne out by the three accounts he left of the interview. The shortest is as explicit as any. 'Ministers said they were determined to evacuate and would I go and superintend it? I said "Yes." '

That evening, January 18, in company with Colonel J D H Stewart of the 11th Hussars, he caught the eight o'clock Continental express. Wolseley carried his solitary kitbag, and emptied his pockets to provide him with money for the journey. Lord Granville took his ticket, and the Duke of Cambridge, who had surprisingly appeared, held open the carriage door for him. Next day the people of Britain breathed more freely; their champion had gone out against the infidel and must assuredly triumph. Queen Victoria with a truer instinct wrote in her diary: 'His attempt is a very dangerous one.'

### III

Two questions must be briefly examined, for on their answer depends our judgment of the protagonists. What precisely was Gordon's mandate in his mission? Was the sending him at all folly or wisdom?

The written instructions which he received after the meeting with Ministers on January 18 empowered him to proceed to Suakim and to report on the military situation in the Soudan and the best means of evacuating Khartoum and the other garrisons. Such had been his original proposal to Wolseley. But at the close they contained the pregnant addendum that he should be under the orders of the British Minister at Cairo and should 'perform such other duties as may be entrusted to him by the Egyptian Government through Sir Evelyn Baring.' This was clearly inserted in deference to Baring's request for a British officer who should conduct the evacuation, and it made the mission executive as well as advisory. The impression left on the Ministers themselves as to what they had done was vague; Northbrook thought that the task included executive powers, Dilke, who was not present all the time, considered that it was only to report. But the written words admit of no doubt, and there was none in Gordon's mind. He held that his mandate had been enlarged since he first talked to Wolseley, and in the official memorandum that he wrote on his journey to Egypt he set out the purpose of his mission thus:

> I understand that Her Majesty's Government have come to the decision not to incur the very onerous duty of securing to the peoples of the Soudan a just future Government. That, as a consequence, Her Majesty's Government have determined to restore to these peoples their independence, and will no longer suffer the Egyptian Government to interfere with their affairs. For this purpose, Her Majesty's Government have decided to send me to the Soudan to arrange for the evacuation of these countries and the safe removal of the Egyptian employees and troops.

In a crisis consistency is not possible for mortals. Baring had been inconsistent, for he began by asking for a British officer for the Soudan, then refused Gordon or any other British officer, and then was compelled by the force of facts to return to his first request. British Ministers had not been consistent, for they had started with a vague idea of a simple mission of inquiry; then under Baring's pressure they had added to Gordon's instructions the duty of taking further orders from their Minister on the spot, and they knew that Baring wanted a man who could act as well as report. The change was right, for when the floods are out a bare report by a hydraulic expert is folly.

But it involved one consequence fraught with future tragedy. The Prime Minister was not present at the War Office meeting. He had had no direct part in the discussion with Gordon, and had still at the back of his mind the idea of an emissary sent only to advise. The Ministers, in spite of a slight confusion of mind, realised that they had done something momentous. 'We were proud of ourselves yesterday,' said one of them to another. 'Are you sure we did not commit a gigantic folly?' Unfortunately, Lord Hartington, in reporting the matter to his chief, did not explain the significant words at the end of the instructions and the importance of Baring's last request. He spoke only of 'advice' and of Gordon's notes of his talk with Wolseley. The Prime Minister concurred, and a few days later in full Cabinet the instructions were ratified. But Mr Gladstone had not grasped the change, and when later he was compelled to accept executive action on Gordon's part he was naturally aggrieved.

He believed that Gordon had forced his hand. He had always been chary of high-coloured adventurers with popular reputations, and he could not forget Gordon's confidences to the dangerous Mr Stead. Here was a man who, given a yard, had taken a mile. He was aware, too, that in his Cabinet was an imperialist section who had very different views from his own, and he feared that they might be using Gordon to coerce him. In his mind were implanted suspicions which were to bear disastrous fruit. But to any candid inquirer it must be clear that Gordon did not go beyond his instructions, or Baring improve upon them. Everything that was done in the following months was covered by the letter of the Government's explicit mandate. And who shall say that the spirit was violated when that spirit was such an obscure and wavering breath?

As to the wisdom of the mission we have the considered verdict of Lord Cromer nearly a quarter of a century later, when he had seen a new Egypt rise under his hand, and could be frank about past blunders. 'Looking back at what occurred after a space of many years,' he wrote, 'two points are to my mind clear. The first is that no Englishman should have been sent to Khartoum. The second is that, if anyone had to be sent, General Gordon was not the right man to send.' On the first point there can be little dispute. If an Englishman was beleaguered in Khartoum it must mean an armed expedition, which was precisely what the British Government desired to avoid. It meant the giving of colossal hostages to fortune, especially if that Englishman were a popular hero. Had an Egyptian or an Arab been sent instead there would no doubt have been an imperfect evacuation – but that was what actually happened. Much bloodshed would have been avoided, and the military and civilian population of Khartoum would have been no worse off in the end. As for the character of the envoy, Lord Cromer's view is coloured by his strong prepossessions against Gordon's type. He admired him but never trusted him, and beyond question he found him a difficult subordinate. He was fond of quoting Gordon's own words in his journal: 'I know if *I* was chief I would never employ *myself*, for I am incorrigible.' But, as a plain matter of fact, putting aside the initial unwisdom of the enterprise, it is doubtful if any other Englishman would have done better. Gordon made mistakes, but so did everybody. Gordon changed his views, but so did Baring. As we shall see, in all major matters the crusading soldier was as staunch a realist as the shrewd diplomatist, and infinitely more so than Her Majesty's Government.

But even to condemn the mission is after-the-event wisdom. We must remember the 'climate of opinion' in which British Ministers were living and the meagre facts which they had at their command. They had Gordon's word for it that the thing was feasible, the word of the chief expert on the Soudan. He gravely underestimated the Mahdi's power, and overestimated his own. The Mahdi was to him a nationalist figure like Arabi, the kind of leader whom all oppressed peoples must sooner or later throw up – a view in which he agreed with Mr Gladstone; in part that, and in part a figurehead set up by discontented slave raiders against the Government. He heard that he was a nephew of a Dongolawi who had once been his guide, and he believed that no great thing could come out of that Nazareth. So far as the movement had a popular appeal he could counter it by his own prestige, offering himself instead of this obscure Wat Tyler as the people's saviour. He had a contempt, too, natural in a man who had been for years working a thousand miles deeper in the heart of Africa, for a leader sprung of the tame riverine tribes. What he did not realise was that behind the Dongolawi was the flame of a religious faith, savage and maleficent, but as fierce and forthright as his own. He communicated to Ministers and officials his own confidence, and his known foibles did not alarm them. He was bold to rashness, but this was a case for that kind of bravery: his religious beliefs, a little disquieting to sober churchmen, would by their very extravagance be a match for the fanaticism of the desert.

There was another reason which weighed heavily with the British Government. Humanity demanded that they should make an effort to rescue those unfortunates whom the folly of Egypt had marooned in the Soudan, since they had assumed responsibility for the guidance of Egypt and therefore for the redress of her blunders. This was felt by British Ministers, who were honourable men, and it was deeply felt by the nation. The flamboyant Mr Stead expounded the views of a multitude of wiser people than himself. The Mahdi and his hordes were thought of as merciless savages, certain, if Khartoum were not evacuated in time, to make a wholesale slaughter of its people. Alike to patriot and humanitarian, to haters of slavery and sticklers for national honour, the situation seemed to call for immediate action. The press agitation may have fanned the flame, but the flame was not basely kindled.

Occasions occur, Lord Cromer has written, 'when the best service a Government official can render to his country is to place himself in opposition to the public view,' and he adds that he never ceased to regret that he had not maintained his original objection to Gordon's mission. But had that objection been maintained it would have been against the evidence of facts and in defiance of what was a proper instinct in the nation. Some attempt had to be made to save the innocent, only an Englishman could make that attempt, and on the facts Gordon, in spite of drawbacks, was the best Englishman. The course of events has shown that it would have been wiser for all concerned to do nothing; but that view in January 1884 would have been a cowardly dereliction of duty. It is better for a nation to play the fool than the knave.

# ACT THE SECOND: THE JOURNEY

## I

As Gordon travelled through France his mind was busy on his task. He drew up and despatched to Lord Granville various proposals, that he should be given his old title of Governor-General of the Soudan that he might act with the greater authority, and that he should issue certain proclamations to the Soudanese people. These the Cabinet accepted, and authorised Baring to give effect to them. While he was crossing the Mediterranean he prepared a further memorandum for Baring. He had not forgotten the latter's desire to leave some rudiments of order after the evacuation, so he suggested that the government should be handed over to the petty sultans whose families had been in power at the time of Mohammed Ali's conquest. In some areas there were no such ruling houses, but the question what to do there could be reserved. On the policy of evacuation he was firm. 'The sacrifice,' he concluded, 'necessary towards securing a good government would be far too onerous to admit of any such attempt being made. Indeed, one may say it is impracticable at any cost. HM's Government will now leave them as God has placed them.'

The original intention had been for Gordon to meet Baring at Ismailia and then proceed direct to Suakim, for he had no wish to see the Khedive, whom he had publicly criticised. But the Suakim area was in confusion, and a force of Egyptian gendarmerie under Valentine Baker had been despatched there. Baring accordingly secured Lord Granville's consent for Gordon to come to Cairo. The change of plan was vital, for had the latter gone to Suakim he would never have got through to Khartoum, and would probably have been back in Egypt within a few weeks. On January 24 a special train decanted at Cairo 'a small man in a black greatcoat, with neither servant nor portmanteau.' Gordon after his fashion stepped modestly on to his new stage.

Next day he saw the Khedive, to whom he apologised for past rudenesses, and the two became friends. To Baring and to Nubar he bore himself with the utmost cordiality. He was in high spirits, and impressed all who met him with his youth and his physical vigour. In long consultations the details of his mission were considered, and those further instructions were drafted which Baring had been empowered by the British Cabinet to give him. The area of evacuation was extended from Khartoum to the whole Soudan. The plan of restoring the petty sultans was approved. It was agreed that the work might take some months, and Gordon was allowed to retain the Egyptian troops for such reasonable period as he might think necessary. He was given a credit of £100,000 and a promise of whatever further funds he might require. A firman appointed him Governor-General of the Soudan, and he was provided by the Khedive with two proclamations which he was to issue at his discretion; one notifying the people of his new rank, and one announcing the evacuation and the 'restoration to the families of the kings of the Soudan of their former independence.'

These details the British Cabinet approved, but they pointed out that they altered Gordon's mission from one of advice to one of executive action. This, as we have seen, was not the case, since the closing sentence of the London instructions effected such a change: of this Lord Granville was perfectly aware, for on January 18 he had telegraphed to Baring about Gordon being 'on his way to Khartoum to arrange for the future settlement of the Soudan for the best advantage of the people.' There might have been some natural doubt in Mr Gladstone's mind, but there could be none in the mind of the Ministers actually concerned.

There was another interview during these days which had fateful consequences. At the house of Chèrif Pasha, the former Prime Minister, Gordon accidentally met Zobeir, the slave dealer of the Bahr-el-Ghazal, who had been living for six years in Cairo. He was Zobeir's sworn enemy, for he had ruined his career and had been indirectly the cause of his son's death, and on his journey to Egypt he had advised Lord Granville to intern him in Cyprus to keep him out of the way of mischief. But the sudden sight of the man gave him a 'mystic feeling' that here was one who might be used as a counterweight to the Mahdi, for he knew his great ability, his stern and ruthless character, and his power with the nomad tribes. He insisted on a second interview, at which Baring and Nubar were present. Zobeir refused to shake hands with him, and loaded him with passionate reproaches for his son's death and the loss of his fortune. Gordon defended himself no less passionately, but the interview ended with some approach to harmony. The impression, however, left upon those present was that if Zobeir were allowed to accompany Gordon there would be murder done in the desert, and Baring refused his consent.

That night Gordon left Cairo with Stewart by train for Assiout, on his way to Khartoum by the Nile valley. He had been a little depressed during the last hours at not getting his way about Zobeir, but he had been cheered by playing with the children of Baring and Evelyn Wood. To the latter's butler he had insisted on presenting his dresscoat and waistcoat, since he would no longer have any need for them. Gerald Graham, his old friend of Crimean and Chinese days, accompanied him as far as Korosko. On the journey Gordon's spirits rose. Before leaving Cairo, he had telegraphed to Khartoum, 'Don't be panic-stricken; you are men, not women; I am coming.' He wrote to his sister, 'I feel quite happy, for if God is with me, who can or will be hurtful to me?' Even the spectacle of his travelling companion, the Emir Abdul

Chakour, did not depress him, though the performance of the ruler-designate of Darfur, smothered in an ill-fitting uniform, attended by a score of wives, and drinking steadily, augured ill for the success of his plan of installing the Soudan's ancient chiefs.

Graham has left us a picture of Gordon in these days, the last glimpse of him permitted to his old friends. He was sometimes preoccupied with his future task, discussing plans for handing over the southern provinces to the King of the Belgians, for relieving Slatin, and for driving the Hadendowa from Suakim. But often he would gossip about his old days in Equatoria, and expound his theories about the Holy Land, and talk bad Arabic to the Nile boatmen. When the time came for the friends to part, Graham walked for a little beside Gordon's camel, while in front rode the Arab escort, armed with rhinoceros-hide shields and great cross-hilted swords. 'At last I left him, saying "Goodbye" and "God bless you." The place where I last saw Gordon is wild and desolate…nothing between the hills but black basins or ravines, dry, dark, and destitute of all vegetation, looking like separate entrances to the pit where those who entered might leave hope behind… I climbed up the highest of these hills, and through a glass watched Gordon and the small caravan as his camels threaded their way along a sandy valley, hoping that he would turn round that I might give him one more sign; but he rode on until he turned the dark side of the hills, and I saw him no more.'

## II

Gordon reached Khartoum on February 18. Much had happened since he left Cairo. Valentine Baker with his rabble of Egyptian gendarmerie had failed against Osman Digna; he had been defeated at El Teb on February 4 with the loss of nearly two-thirds of his force, including eleven European officers. The garrison of Sinkat had been overpowered and massacred; Tokar was in hourly danger of falling; and Suakim itself was threatened. Immediately a clamour arose in England for a relief expedition to the eastern

Soudan. There were meetings throughout the country, the anti-slavery forces were mobilised, and Mr W E Forster, who had resigned from the Cabinet two years before, trenchantly attacked the Government. Embarrassed Ministers were forced to a decision.

Had they been consistent they would have left the protection of Suakim to the British Fleet, and declared that, since they had despatched Gordon on a general mission of evacuation, it was not their business to concern themselves with isolated garrisons, and that in any case they were firm against any military expedition. Mr Gladstone took this view, but he was overruled. Gordon, who was consulted by telegram, was reluctant to assent to the use of force. But the debate in the House of Commons on February 12 revealed a strong feeling for immediate intervention, and it was decided to send Sir Gerald Graham at once to Suakim with an army of British regulars. The decision was fateful. The British Government had of their own initiative, and under no pressure from Gordon, abandoned their policy of a wholly peaceful evacuation. If Gordon later asked for British troops he was only following the lead of his superiors. Ministers had been rudely shaken out of their frugal optimism.

Meantime on his journey south Gordon's eyes were being opened to the immense difficulties of his mission. It was his habit, which he had acquired under Ismail, to put his views at once on paper and communicate them to his chiefs, even though he might change his opinion radically once a week. This method enabled them to see the processes of his mind. But in a land where transport was difficult the custom had its drawbacks, for it meant often that an early message arrived after a later one, and the recipient was left in confusion. He was clear about his two tasks, to evacuate the garrisons and to leave behind some makeshift system of law and order. Baring had been as insistent upon the second as upon the first. It was this latter that most troubled him. The alcoholic Abdul Chakour had disillusioned him about his plan of setting up in power the old Soudanese families. He must leave

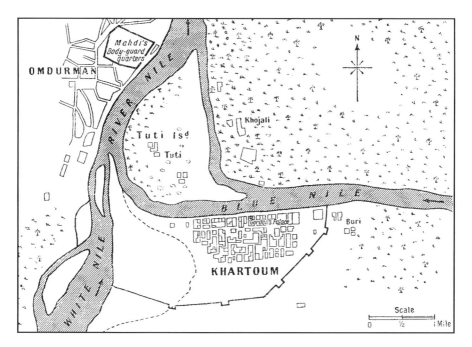

PLAN OF KHARTOUM

a man behind him, a man fit to govern and to defy the Mahdi, and his mind returned again to his old enemy Zobeir. Something also might be done with the King of the Belgians; if King Leopold took over the Equatorial provinces he himself might go south when his work in Khartoum was over and take service under him. He had an idea, too, of paying a personal visit to the Mahdi, and reasoning with that disturber of the peace. All these views he communicated seriatim to the puzzled Baring.

At Berber he summoned a council of notables, and showed them the Khedive's firman announcing Egypt's withdrawal from the Soudan. It was a dangerous step. On January 8 he had told the *Pall Mall Gazette*: 'There is one subject which I cannot imagine anyone differing about. That is the impolicy of announcing our intention to evacuate Khartoum. The moment it is known we have given up the game, every man will go over to the Mahdi. All men worship the rising sun.' No doubt he had good reason for his action, but it would appear that later he came to doubt its wisdom.

The truth is that he still underestimated the Mahdi's power, thinking him no more than a local upstart. He sent him robes of honour and offered him his friendship and the rank of Sultan of Kordofan; the Mahdi replied with point that he was already Sultan of Kordofan and much more, and returned the compliment by sending a patched jibbah and inviting his opponent to turn Moslem and save his wretched soul. At Berber Gordon did another thing which made a great outcry in England. The Anglo-Egyptian Convention of 1877 would bring slavery in the Soudan to an end in 1889. When the notables asked him if this provision would apply, he replied that it would not, since the Soudan was now independent of Egypt, and he issued a proclamation to that effect. It was obvious common sense, but it alienated some of his noisier supporters at home.

At half-past nine on the morning of February 18 Gordon landed at Khartoum at the stage opposite the palace. Thousands pressed about him to kiss his hands and feet. He struck while the iron was hot. First he made a bonfire of old instruments of oppression, the books of the tax-gatherers, the bonds of the usurers, and the kourbashes of the police. In the gaols fetters were removed from the limbs of prisoners. Certain Egyptian units he despatched at once to Cairo, and he formed a council of Arab notables. 'I come,' he told the people, 'without soldiers, but with God on my side, to redeem the evils of the Soudan. I will not fight with any weapon but justice.' The city rang all day with plaudits and blazed all night with fires of joy. Gordon had touched the heart and kindled the spirit of the mixed multitude within the walls.

As he looked round him his mind was divided between hope and fear. He believed that the Mahdi's levies would only fight within tribal limits, and that if he could hold the tribes between Khartoum and Egypt the evacuation was safe. By his concessions he thought that this might be possible, for the news of his first deeds in the city would soon be spread over the land. But for the rest? Of one capital danger he had as yet no knowledge. The news of his safe arrival had enabled the British Government to rebut triumphantly the vote of censure, but the Cabinet had relapsed in their relief into a mood of stubborn illogicality. They would send British soldiers under Graham to Suakim, because Suakim belonged to Egypt and they were responsible for Egypt. But, though the Red Sea coast was nominally part of the Soudan, it was somehow different from the rest, and they would admit of no armed intervention in the Soudan. 'I contend,' said Lord Hartington with a fine inconsequence on the last day of the debate, 'that we are not responsible for the rescue or relief of the garrisons either in the Western or the Southern or the Eastern Soudan.' At first, in their anxiety during Gordon's journey across the desert, Hartington, Duke and Chamberlain had been ready to press for British troops to support him, and, if necessary, relieve him, but now all three had been shepherded back to Mr Gladstone's fold. Daily the Prime Minister was growing more malcontent with the mission and more suspicious of the missionary.

The vacillation of London was mercifully hid from Gordon's knowledge, but he had one gnawing anxiety ever present – the future ordering of the Soudan, which even the cautious Baring had considered a primal duty. His imagination swept over the vast country, noting the tiny 'pin-point garrisons, each smothered in a cloud of Arab spears.' By his proclamation he had given this land back to its people, but what could they make of it? Someone must exercise a nominal sovereignty. Egypt could not; Turkey would not; then Britain must. Why not establish a buffer state like Afghanistan, where Britain was not responsible for the government but gave moral support and a subsidy? But if a second Afghanistan was created, there must be an Amir – someone to succeed himself as Governor-General. For that post there was only one man, Zobeir. On the day of his arrival in Khartoum Gordon telegraphed to Baring urging this plan, and Stewart sent a telegram in its support. He had not changed his mind, and enlarged his mandate;

he was only proposing means for carrying out the second and, as he considered, equally vital part of his orders.

III

If the Zobeir question is to be fairly judged, the different points of view must be remembered, for it is not a case for sweeping conclusions. Gordon's mind had been made up on the matter ever since his arrival in Cairo, and his 'mystical feeling' about the ex-slave trader had been reinforced by what he had learned on his journey to Khartoum. Zobeir, he was convinced, was the only man capable of holding his own against the Mahdi, and, when Khartoum was evacuated, of preventing the Soudan from becoming a cockpit. He had been the conqueror of Darfur and was a born ruler of men. He was of the blood of the Koreish, a descendant of the Abbaside dynasty, and had therefore an ancestral religious authority which with Moslem fanatics might outweigh the Mahdi's spurious claims. He was feared by the commonalty, but, as Baring discovered thirteen years later, he was also revered. Zobeir alone could fulfil what he believed to be an integral part of his own instructions, and preserve order when he had gone. As for the personal vendetta he would take the risk. These considerations he pressed upon Baring in the long telegram which he despatched as soon as he arrived in Khartoum.

Baring to his credit was open to conviction. He, too, realised the need of finding a successor to Gordon, for he had never wavered about the duty of establishing some post-evacuation authority. He was prepared to accept Zobeir under strict conditions, not to provide 'moral support' but to announce the British Government's 'approbation'; he thought that there was something in the Afghanistan precedent. He accordingly urged the appointment upon Lord Granville, who replied discouragingly. Gordon was informed, and answered that he could suggest no other name to meet the case. He added some sentences of prescient wisdom, but of doubtful prudence in view of the mood of the Home Government:

> My duty is evacuation, and the best I can for establishing a quiet Government. The first I hope to accomplish. The second is a more difficult task and concerns Egypt more than me. If Egypt is to be quiet Mahdi must be smashed up... Remember that once Khartoum belongs to Mahdi, the task will be far more difficult, yet you will, for safety of Egypt, execute it. If you decide on smashing Mahdi, then send up another £100,000, and send up 200 Indian troops to Wadi Halfa and leave Suakim and Massowah alone. I repeat that evacuation is possible, but you will feel effect in Egypt, and will be forced to enter into a far more serious affair to guard Egypt. At present it would be comparatively easy to destroy Mahdi.

After events were to justify every word of this message, but the effect on the British Cabinet was disastrous. To Ministers it seemed that Gordon had gone far beyond his powers, and was changing his views with a disquieting speed. First, on the Zobeir question. He had wanted Zobeir exiled to Cyprus; he now wished him to be a kind of Afghan Amir in the Soudan. Baring had telegraphed on February 28: 'Whatever may be said to the contrary, Her Majesty's Government must be in reality responsible for any arrangements which can be devised for the Soudan, and I do not think it is possible to shake off the responsibility.' Dare they take on themselves the burden of Zobeir's appointment? Not even Gordon's name would sweeten the pill to a suspicious public. The Anti-Slavery Society would arise in its wrath, and a watchful Opposition would seize the chance to wreck the Government.

Two Cabinet meetings considered the matter, the Prime Minister being absent. Three Ministers were in favour of Zobeir on general grounds, but all were clear that the House of Commons would never permit it. The question was raised there, and Mr W

E Forster fulminated against the proposal. The Liberal press was furiously hostile, the Conservative press critical. Mr Gladstone alone supported it. Coming of a family which had owned many slaves, he had not in his blood that detestation of the very name of slavery which most Englishmen possessed; he saw, too, in Zobeir's appointment a means of bringing to an end the perilous mission of a man whom every day he distrusted more profoundly. But he was overcome by the argument about the hostility of Parliament, though he believed that had he himself been able to be in his place he might have swung the House to his side. A year later he said: 'It is well known that if, when the recommendation to send Zobeir was made, we had complied with it, an address from this House to the Crown would, before forty-eight hours were over, have paralysed our action; and although it is perfectly true that the decision arrived at was the judgment of the Cabinet, it was also no less the judgment of Parliament and of the people.' So far as it goes the defence is sound. No British Government could have sent Zobeir to the Soudan and survived for a week. Gordon continued to plead for him, and Baring to press for him with all the weight of the man on the spot, but on March 11 the Cabinet finally refused.

Had Gordon's proposal been accepted, would Khartoum have been saved? Lord Cromer believed that it might. To me it seems more than doubtful, for Zobeir with all his power would have found himself faced by something greater than himself, an incalculable, whirlwind, fanatic horde drunk with visions of Paradise. Nevertheless it is likely that if he had gone south at once he would have delayed the attack long enough to permit of at least a partial evacuation and to ensure Gordon's own safety. But for that he should have left Cairo before the end of February: by March 11, when the British Cabinet decided, it was already too late.

The difference over Zobeir was only one of the grounds of quarrel between Gordon and his superiors at home. Far graver was the effect of his other message, which to Ministers seemed to imply an amazing fickleness of mind and a determination not to evacuate but to conquer. He had proposed a friendly visit to the Mahdi, and then wanted to make him Sultan of Kordofan; now he was eager to smash him. He had wanted Suakim to be left alone, and now he proposed that the Suakim-Berber route should be opened and British troops sent to the latter place. He was announcing to the people of Khartoum that British soldiers were on their way; he was talking wildly of breaking through to Equatoria. Clearly he was trying to force Britain into a military adventure. Ministers could not make allowances (even Baring found it difficult) for a man who telegraphed whenever an idea struck him, and for the desperate expedients of one confronted with an insoluble problem. They did not know, as we know now, that all the while Gordon was labouring at the hopeless task of evacuation, that he had already got rid of the sick and feeble, and that it was principally to help him in that work that he suggested the sending of British or Indian troops to Wadi Halfa and Berber. The short-range imagination of Ministers prevented them from grasping the rudiments of his difficulties. Even Duke and Chamberlain turned against him, and Mr Gladstone's attitude became that of the whole Cabinet. He had lost their confidence, and therefore it was their plain duty to recall him. They did not do this, for they feared the people, and presently it was too late.

For on March 12, the day after the Cabinet had finally refused him Zobeir, a force of 4000 Arabs came down upon the Nile nine miles north of Khartoum, cut the telegraph line, and blocked all movement to and from Egypt. Zobeir might have prevented it, but there was no Zobeir. What was at stake now was not the success of the mission but the life of the envoy.

# ACT THE THIRD: THE FORLORN HOPE

## I

From the first day of his arrival at Khartoum Gordon set himself to his primary task, the business of evacuation. He separated the Egyptian from the Soudanese troops, for the latter must be retained as a police force for Zobeir or whoever was to take charge of the Soudan. The former he removed across the river to Omdurman to await transport to Berber. He asked Baring to make provision for their reception at Korosko, and arranged with his agent at Berber for the despatch of boats southwards. The sick and the widows and orphans were sent away at once. Altogether some 600 soldiers and 2000 civilians were evacuated. His duty was to perform the task without use of force, and at first it looked as if his personal prestige would achieve this end. The people of Khartoum were docile in his hands. Women flocked round him begging him to touch and cure their children, and he was hailed as Father and Saviour. For a moment it seemed as if the Mahdi's spell was to be nullified by a greater. Even the Khartoum notables, who were nervous about the removal of the Egyptian troops, were silenced by his serene faith.

But the main problem was not the people of Khartoum but the neighbouring tribes, and here dangers at once presented themselves. The Mahdi's emissaries were busy among them, and the Egyptian posts on both the Blue and the White Nile were threatened.

Gordon was compelled to send a small relief expedition which did not fire a shot, but distributed his peace proclamations, what he called his 'paper warfare.' News travels fast in the desert, and his pacific overtures were not helped by what was happening on the Red Sea littoral. Sir Gerald Graham with British troops had defeated Osman Digna at El Teb, and a little later at Tamaai he completed the dispersal of the rebels in that area. Thousands of the Hadendowa tribe lay dead on the field, but it was a meaningless and a fruitless slaughter. It complicated Gordon's task at Khartoum, and Graham's success only made the situation worse unless it meant that the Suakim-Berber route would be opened and British troops would appear on the Nile. The British Government had no such intention. To defeat the Mahdi's eastern levies with British regiments was apparently in their eyes a pacific business, but to send a handful of British soldiers to keep the Nile open for the accomplishment of the duty which they had laid upon their envoy would have been a shameful and perilous act of war.

Yet Berber was the key of the whole enterprise. If the river route to the north was blocked a peaceful evacuation would be impossible, and already the dervishes were drifting Nile-wards. Gordon, busy with the evacuation at the Khartoum end, pled with Baring to send him Zobeir, and to despatch a British contingent, however small, to Berber to hold that key-point. From Berber the refugees must go either by river to Abu Hamed and then by the desert route to Korosko, or straight to Suakim, and in either case the neutrality of the local tribes must be assured. This seemed so self-evident that he could not believe that his request would not be granted, for surely a Government that willed the end would will the only means. If not, he told Baring, there was nothing for it but that Khartoum should be given up, that Stewart should take the Egyptian troops and employees to Berber and try to hold the place, and that he himself should resign his commission and retire with the remaining steamers and stores to Equatoria.

Baring was in a hopeless position. Every morning he found a sheaf of telegrams from Gordon, which were virtually a diary of the thoughts that had passed through his mind. To the recipient they seemed a tangle of confusion, but he had the wit to see the inexorable facts. Gordon was in a dilemma which fate, not himself, had created. The question was rapidly becoming not whether Khartoum could be successfully evacuated, but whether Gordon and Stewart could be got away. Since Zobeir was refused him, the only hope lay in a dash across the desert to Berber by some of Graham's cavalry so as to impress the tribes and make the place defensible. Military opinion in Egypt was on the whole against this, and the Home Government seized the excuse to veto the plan. On March 26 Baring put before Lord Granville his considered view, the view of a cool and impartial mind:

> Let me earnestly beg Her Majesty's Government to put themselves in the position of Gordon and Stewart. They have been sent on a most difficult and dangerous mission by the English Government. Their proposal to send Zobeir, which, if it had been acted on some weeks ago, would certainly have entirely altered the situation, was rejected. The consequences which they foresaw have ensued… Coetlogon, who is here, assures me that so long as the rebels hold both banks of the river above the Sixth Cataract, it will be quite impossible for boats to pass. He does not believe that Gordon can cut his way through by land. He ridicules the idea of retreating with the garrison to Equatoria, and we may be sure that Gordon and Stewart will not come away alone. As a matter of personal opinion, I do not believe in the impossibility of helping Gordon, even during the summer, if Indian troops are employed and money is not spared. But if it be decided to make no attempt to afford present help, then I would urge that Gordon be told to try and maintain his position during the summer, and that then, if he is still beleaguered, an expedition will be sent as early as possible in the autumn to relieve him. This would, at all events, give him some hope, and the mere announcement of the intention of the

Government would go a long way to ensure his safety by keeping loyal tribes who may be still wavering. No one regrets more than I do the necessity of sending British or Indian troops to the Soudan, but, having sent Gordon to Khartoum, it appears to me that it is our bounden duty, both as a matter of humanity and policy, not to abandon him.

Meantime since March 12 the telegraph line had been cut, the river route blocked, and Khartoum in a state of siege. Baring's messages could only reach Gordon from Berber by slow and devious ways, and Gordon's could only get to Cairo by being carried on small strips of paper by native runners through the enemy lines. The result was that they arrived irregularly and many did not arrive at all. A thick mist had crept between Khartoum and the outer world.

## II

All through March and well into April Gordon believed that Zobeir would be given him and that a small detachment of British troops would be sent to keep the Nile route open. Graham's operations in the eastern Soudan had greatly increased the difficulties with the local tribes; but he could not believe that if British soldiers could be used around Suakim, which was not a vital point, they could not be used to assist the central duty of his mission. Knowing the desert as no other man knew it, he was convinced that a light force could cover the 250 miles between Suakim and Berber, the same distance as separated the Mahdi's headquarters at El Obeid from Khartoum. For three weeks he never fired a shot. Then he was forced to defend himself, for on all sides, from south and west and east and north, the enemy began to close in on him. Dervish bullets were killing men at the palace windows. He wrote that he was as safe as if he was in Cairo, but that was only the bravado of a good soldier. He knew that he was defending a forlorn hope, that he had with him a feeble garrison and many thousands of helpless civilians, and that at home there was a Government which could not grasp the truth.

During the long summer months he received only belated and disjointed news from Baring, and he could not be certain that his pleas for help – for Turkish troops, if British were not forthcoming, or for a levy of adventurers financed by private friends – ever reached their destination. He could not conceive that Britain would forsake him, and he had a fixed hope of a relief expedition when the Nile rose. The few messages that reached him from the north infuriated him by their apparent blindness to the crisis, and he raged against diplomatists and politicians and all their works. But in the meantime he gave every power of mind and body to the task of performing the impossible. In all the history of war there are few records in which the spirit of man shines so triumphantly as in Gordon's desperate toil at the defence of a sprawling city and a scared people, with dwindling supplies and raw troops that drew their only virtue from his courage.

His first duty was to strengthen the ramparts so that the place could not be taken by a sudden assault. On the north and west was the river; east and south he completed the half-moon of fortifications, extending from the Blue to the White Nile at a distance of about two miles from the city. Here the former officer of engineers was in his element. He had redoubts at the eastern angle, at a point about a mile to the west of Khartoum, on the south bank of the Blue Nile, and on the north bank south of Khojali. He held also the mud town of Omdurman as an outpost on the west bank of the White Nile. He supported the defence with an elaborate system of wire entanglements and land mines, which latter had a tremendous moral effect upon the attacking dervishes. Having the resources of the old Egyptian arsenal at his disposal, he was also able to armour his steamers so as to enable them to run the gauntlet of rifle fire from the shores. The rising of the Nile towards the end of April provided him with a new protection on the west, for now a broad lagoon lay between him and Kordofan. He had been doubtful from the first about his

Egyptian troops. In March a handful of Arabs had put a thousand of them to flight, and he had court-martialled and shot the two officers responsible – an act which he bitterly regretted afterwards, but one which doubtless tightened discipline. Slowly he built up a more effective force of volunteers, chiefly of Negro slaves, and he put a Negro, Faragh Pasha, in command. By the end of April he had beaten off the first dervish attack, and won a breathing space.

He was also civil governor and had to order the life of the beleaguered city. He sent out expeditions far and wide to collect food, and, though Coetlogon in March had estimated that there were supplies for no more than one month, he managed to hold out for ten. Not only did he feed the people, but he nursed their spirit. He told the ulemas what they should preach, and, stern disciplinarian as he was, he was gentle to the *bouches inutiles* and bore in public always a smiling face. Though he toiled to the last limit of human power, he made it his habit to appear unruffled and confident. He slept mainly in the afternoon, for most of the night he was up and visiting the ramparts. 'I am always frightened,' he told a friend. 'It is not the fear of death – that is past, thank God, but I fear defeat and its consequences. I do not believe in the calm, unmoved man.' But the anxious inhabitants saw only a serene competence; he kept his exasperation and his fears for his messages to Cairo. No detail of the city's life escaped his notice. He issued paper notes, he manufactured and awarded decorations, and he supervised to the last ounce the issue of food.

The besiegers were kept at a respectful distance, but every day shots from Khojali fell into Khartoum, and soon ill news came from further afield. At the end of April a post on the Blue Nile, halfway to Sennar, was forced to surrender with large quantities of food and rifles and one of his precious steamers. On May 27 Berber fell, and five thousand of its people were massacred. The place had ceased to be the key of the evacuation, since that had long ago become an impossibility, but it remained a strategic point for any British advance, and it was never out of Gordon's mind.

He dreamed of so strengthening his position that he would be able to send an expedition to recapture Berber, and then join hands with the British advance which must be now beginning. At the end of June he scornfully rejected a demand from the Mahdi for his surrender. 'The Mohammedans who are with me do not wish to surrender, and do you expect that I, who am a Christian, should set the example?' On July 13 he sent out a batch of messages by native runners, five of which reached the outer world by the end of August, to say that Khartoum could hold out for four months. In July and August things went better for the defence. Gordon's ablest native officer, Mohammed Ali, won a victory on the Blue Nile and cleared a considerable extent of country, while another victory at Halfaya opened up part of the road to the north. He had plans now for the recapture of Berber, and informed Baring that he would send an expedition under Stewart for that purpose, and would hold the town till reinforcements came – or burn it and fall back.

It was the gleam of sunshine before the storm. Before moving on Berber it seemed wise to meet a new enemy threat twenty-five miles up the Blue Nile. Mohammed Ali, in his desire to capture the dervish chief, was betrayed into an ambush in difficult country, and perished with a thousand of his men. Gordon had to revise his plan, for the Nile would soon be beginning to fall, leaving Khartoum more exposed on the Kordofan side, and he could not afford to deplete his garrison. The messages, too, that were coming through from Cairo showed him that England was grossly ignorant of his plight, and he began to fear for that British advance upon which he had based all his hopes. He resolved to make a desperate effort to let the truth be known. Stewart should go down the river to Dongola with despatches. He wrote his last letter to Baring:

How many times have we written for reinforcements, calling your serious attention to the Soudan! No answer at all has come to us...and the hearts of men have become weary at this delay. While you are eating and drinking and resting on good beds, we and those with us, soldiers and servants, are watching by night and day, endeavouring to quell the movements of this false Mahdi… The reason why I have now sent Colonel Stewart is because you have been silent all this while and neglected us, and lost time without doing any good. If troops were sent, as soon as they reach Berber this rebellion will cease.

Tragically, Gordon thought that the chief cause of his predicament was the one man who had been loyal to him from the day he reached Cairo, and had damaged his prestige with the British Cabinet by telling it unwelcome truths.

Stewart, accompanied by the *Times* correspondent and the French consul, set out in the *Abbas*, escorted by two other steamers to see him past the danger-point of Berber, and a couple of feluccas. Berber was safely passed, and then unfortunately Stewart decided to send the escort back. When within two days of Dongola the *Abbas* struck a rock in midstream. Natives appeared on the bank with a white flag, and the three Europeans, believing them friendly, landed to parley with them. There they met a local sheikh, who invited them into a house, where they were instantly murdered. Gordon's diary and the key to his cyphers were captured and despatched to the Mahdi.

It was a grievous mischance, and it sealed the fate of Khartoum. Had Stewart travelled another hundred miles he would have met a man who would have learned from him of Gordon's desperate straits and would have hurried on the relief. A certain Major Kitchener had the year before been appointed second-in-command of the Egyptian cavalry, and was now doing intelligence work, his business being to keep open the Nubian desert for a possible British advance. He was a tall, very lean man, with long legs and narrow sloping shoulders, a square head, a cast in his left eye, and a face so tanned that his big fair moustache looked almost white. Sir Samuel Baker thought well of him, and Gordon, for whom he was to be soon the only link with the outer world, would have made him Governor-General of the Soudan. As fortune willed, this young sapper officer was in the plenitude of time to be his successor and his avenger.

It was two months before Gordon heard of the disaster to the *Abbas*. When Stewart left on September 9 he had no friends to talk to, so he began that journal of his innermost thoughts which has been preserved for men to read. He knew that the last struggle was approaching, for news had come that the Mahdi was on the move. The victories of the infidel on the Blue Nile had convinced Mohammed Ahmed that he could no longer afford to neglect Khartoum. He had no love of violent assaults, for he had heard of Gordon's land mines, but with his myriads he could encompass the place and starve it into surrender. Wad-el-Nejumi, one of his best captains, was entrusted with the task: he would command the fighting force, but the Mahdi himself would hallow the attack by his presence. Some 200,000 dervishes swarmed eastward from El Obeid, retracing the road which Hicks Pasha had marched to his doom. Being a cautious and sanguine visionary, the Mahdi made fresh efforts to induce his antagonist to do as Slatin and Cuzzi had done, and sent emissaries to summon him to repent and embrace the true faith.

Gordon rejoiced at the coming of his enemy, for it meant that before long the issue would be determined. 'I have always felt,' he wrote in his journal, 'we were doomed to come face to face ere the matter was ended.' Either British troops would arrive in time, or there would be that other release for which he had always longed. The sight of the hawks circling over the palace gave him strange thoughts of approaching death... Soon he heard a sound other than the rattle of Arab sniping. The blowing of the ivory trumpets and the roll of the great copper war-drums told him that his master-foe was near. In numbers like a flight of locusts, the straw bonnets and the patched jibbahs, the black flags and the green, the bright spears and the long swords had come out of the west.

# IRONIC INTERLUDE

The Cabinet meeting of March 11 which refused Zobeir inaugurated five months of dire misunderstanding. British Ministers had argued themselves into two convictions: that Gordon had illegitimately extended his mandate and had thereby relieved them from responsibility for his fate; and that he could leave Khartoum if he chose, and only stayed there because of his obsession by wild dreams of conquest. The answer to the first lay in the letter of the documents, to which they were strangely blind. The answer to the second was to be found in Baring's repeated solemn warnings, though these were to some extent discounted in their mind by the confident tone of the few messages which came through from Khartoum. The Cabinet, with no experience of wild lands and with little imagination, seemed incapable of realising the situation in the Soudan or the plight of their envoy. Military opinion assured them that it was impossible to send British troops from Suakim to Berber, and in any case they believed that it was unnecessary. Not even Baring's urgent telegram of March 26 could move them. 'He makes a recommendation,' the Prime Minister informed the Queen, 'that amounts to a reversal of policy; he overrides the most serious military difficulties; he acts, so far as it appears, alone; he proposes to provide for dangers to General Gordon, of the existence of which at the present moment Your Majesty's Government do not possess evidence; and he does this in ignorance of what are at the time General Gordon's circumstances, opinions and desires.' That is to say, they declined to accept the evidence of the one man who might be supposed to understand the case, and who had never given them cause to suspect him of lightness of mind.

The decision of the Cabinet was unanimous, but some of its members were perturbed in spirit. The radical section was indeed heartily behind the Prime Minister. Sir William Harcourt, the Home Secretary, had threatened to resign if there was any talk of an expedition. Mr Chamberlain had at first been uneasy, and had had the notion of sending Dilke to Egypt to find out the truth, but by the end of March he had come to share Mr Gladstone's view. Lord Granville was well content to do nothing. But Lord Selborne, the Lord Chancellor, had shown signs of revolt unless an expedition was promised for the autumn, and Lord Hartington cannot have been comfortable. Six months later, on September 24, he wrote of Gordon to Lord Granville: 'We have no proof that he could have done anything different from what he has done and is doing, or that he has wilfully disregarded our instructions.' Something of that sort must have been in his mind in March, but Lord Hartington's ideas took a long time to solidify into convictions.

On April 3 the Prime Minister returned to the House of Commons after a slight illness, and the question of the Soudan was raised by Sir Stafford Northcote on the adjournment. Mr Gladstone repeated that Gordon's mission, so far as the British Government was concerned, was advisory and not executive, and he hotly denied the report of the *Times* correspondent that he had been abandoned. Gordon, he announced, had permission to leave Khartoum if he so desired. He lashed the Opposition for taking their information from journalistic tattle, and declared that discussions on Egypt, when there were so many weightier matters on hand, were simply a waste of parliamentary time. The speech was a debating success, and it ravished the soul of Sir William Harcourt. A few days later the latter described the occasion to his constituents in his familiar vein of pious truculence. 'He (Mr Gladstone) had been ill, and they thought that they could play tricks with the sick lion; but they were mistaken. He just put out his paw and there was an end of them. It was a wonderful scene. I have never seen the like of it in my political life. With his unparalleled eloquence he withered them with the blast of his scornful indignation, and he laid bare their inmost souls.' The speech scarcely deserved these heroics. It was based upon fallacies which Baring had exposed, and deductions for which there was no warrant. The word 'abandonment' which stung the Prime Minister was strictly justified.

Mr Gladstone was less fortunate in his defence when the House met again after the Easter recess. The idea of a relief expedition was beginning to creep into the air, private instructions had been sent by the military authorities to make inquiries about the best routes, and the possibility of such a course being forced on him stiffened the old man's temper. He had made up his mind that he would not be coerced by an insubordinate envoy, by the British representative in Cairo whose good sense had unaccountably failed him, by imperialist colleagues, or by sentimental public opinion; and, according to his habit, he seized upon any plea to justify his obstinacy. On April 21 he told the House of Commons that Gordon was 'hemmed in' but not 'surrounded' – a distinction the meaning of which was a secret between himself and his Maker. On April 23 he declared that there was 'no military or other danger threatening Khartoum.' A relief expedition would be needless, impossible, and immoral. It maddened him to think that with so many grave preoccupations the Government should be harassed by this gadfly. The situation with Russia in Central Asia was full of menace. Germany under Bismarck was waiting maliciously to catch Britain at a disadvantage. Any forward move in Egypt would make trouble with France, and a good understanding with Paris was a primary aim of his foreign policy. Besides there were difficult times ahead at home. Ireland was a powder magazine waiting the spark, and over his cherished Franchise Bill he was having trouble with the House of Lords. The Prime Minister had many excuses for his irritation. A little firmness, he decided, and the agitation would die, for stalwarts, like Mr John Morley, believed that people were growing tired of Gordon. There were even soldiers who looked askance at him; it was reported that Sir Redvers Buller, when a dash across the desert was proposed, had declared that 'the man was not worth the camels.'

But when on May 12 a vote of censure was moved in the Commons, he found that all his parliamentary arts were insufficient to allay the anxiety of members, not only of the Opposition, but of his own party. He repeated the familiar arguments – orders disobeyed, messages unanswered, no immediate danger. To send an army to Khartoum would be 'a war of conquest against a people rightly struggling to be free' – a description which future events were to render fantastic in the extreme, since within ten years those aspirants after liberty caused seventy-five per cent of the Soudan population to perish. He was answered with effect by Mr W E Forster, and only Lord Hartington's foreshadowing of an autumn expedition saved the Government from defeat. The bitter comment of Lord Randolph Churchill on Mr Gladstone's speech showed how alien it was to the temper of the House. 'I compared his efforts in the cause of Gordon with his efforts in the cause of Mr Bradlaugh. If one hundredth part of those valuable moral qualities bestowed upon the cause of a seditious blasphemer had been given to the support of a Christian hero, the success of Gordon's mission would have been assured. But the finest speech he ever delivered in the House of Commons was in support of the seditious blasphemer; and the very worst he ever delivered, by common consent, was in the cause of the Christian hero.'

At the end of April Baring was brought to London for a financial conference, but during his two months at home he was unable to make the Government understand the facts. It would appear that they considered their Egyptian duties to be fulfilled for the moment by attending to Egypt's finances. The question of Gordon received only a perfunctory five minutes at the end of the

Cabinet meetings. The Government continued to ask him for full reports on his exact situation, and when they got no answer, since their requests never reached him, decided that he was insubordinate or sulky. They wanted to know the reason why he did not leave Khartoum; the formidable reason was Mohammed Ahmed. They took no steps about the relief expedition which Lord Hartington had hinted at, except to make a few inquiries about routes, though, if such an expedition was to start in the early autumn, the preparations for it should have begun in May. They were determined to wait and see, confident that Gordon could at any time escape if he wished. So no doubt he could. It would have been possible for him with the help of friendly natives to slip through the lines of the besiegers, but he would have left to their fate the people of Khartoum who had given him their trust. 'How could I look the world in the face if I abandoned them and fled?' he had written to Baring. If a desirable quality in an envoy is concern for his own skin, it is unwise to select a soldier – still less a crusader.

The temper of the country was rising. On July 24 Wolseley, with the authority of Britain's most successful soldier, protested strongly against this insane procrastination. Before the end of June the news of the fall of Berber had reached England, and by July 20 at long last a message came through from Gordon, dated June 23, asking for word of the relief expedition. To this the Government only replied by demanding more information as to the situation in Khartoum – a piece of futility which ultimately reached Gordon, but which fortunately he could not read, his cyphers having been lost with Stewart. On July 25 the Cabinet met, and the main business was the question of an expedition. To Mr Gladstone's chagrin only Sir William Harcourt, Lord Kimberley and Lord Granville among his colleagues stood out against it. But he himself was immovable, and he would not bow to the majority's view. More than ever he was determined that a refractory subordinate of a melodramatic turn of mind should not dictate to a British Prime Minister. Besides he was sallying forth to do battle with the House of Lords over his Franchise Bill, and the faithful Mr John Morley was delighting Liberal audiences with delicious witticisms about 'mending or ending' that chamber. No distraction must be permitted in so high a task.

But Mr Gladstone was first and foremost a politician, and on the last day of July he saw reason to change his mind. On the 29th Lord Selborne and Lord Hartington circulated memoranda to the Cabinet urging immediate action. On the 31st the latter announced that an expedition must forthwith be authorised or he would resign his office. The slow mind which had been long in travail had at last given birth to a decision. The Prime Minister, insensible to the persuasion of facts, bowed before party exigencies. He knew that when Lord Hartington spoke of 'a question of personal honour and good faith,' he meant business, for he was not wont to use these spacious words. He knew that the defection of the head of the house of Cavendish would bring down his Government and rend his party. He surrendered at discretion. On August 5 he himself moved in the House of Commons for a grant of funds 'to undertake operations for the relief of General Gordon, should they become necessary, and to make certain preparations in respect thereof.' That day the War Office set to work on plans, and on September 9 Wolseley arrived in Cairo.

Mr Gladstone had yielded, but without conviction. Public opinion at the time saddled him with the guilt of what was to prove a fatal delay, and beyond doubt it was the prepotent force of his character that kept the Cabinet inert. But, since a man is what God made him, it seems to me that the major part of the blame should rest on Lord Hartington for his tardy resolution. Lord Hartington from the first more or less understood the situation, which the Prime Minister never did. Mr Gladstone's mind was cast in a rigid, antique mould, and he would not yield on a principle except in the last necessity. He detested war, both for its own sake, and because it meant a diversion of national interest from what he regarded as worthier matters; he would only sanction it if the need were proved to the hilt, and the kind of evidence which he considered essential was not forthcoming. He had no instinct for things which cannot be formulated in black and white, and no imagination to construct a true picture out of scattered details.

Gordon in his journal on September 23 set down with uncanny intuition his habit of mind. 'It is as if a man on the bank, having seen his friend in the river already bobbed down two or three times, hails: "I say, old fellow, let me know when we are to throw you the lifebuoy. I know you have bobbed down two or three times, but it is a pity to throw you the lifebuoy until you are really *in extremis*, and I want to know exactly, for I am a man brought up in a school of exactitude." ' Facts, when they ran counter to Mr Gladstone's wishes, had to be massed in overwhelming myriads before he could realise them. He was not unlike the Lord Aberdeen of the Crimean War.

The truth is that he had no single gift of the man of action, except in the sheltered arena of domestic politics. Nearly a quarter of a century earlier Lord Salisbury in a *Quarterly* article had acutely diagnosed one part of his psychology. 'His mind, with all its power, has this strange peculiarity that his reason will not work vigorously on any question in which he does not take a hearty interest; and he can only take a hearty interest in one question at one time. On any question therefore, which crosses the subject of his heart...his perceptions are blunted and his reason will not work true.' Again, he wholly lacked the gift of reading characters different from his own and appraising situations outside his narrow experience. Gordon from the start had been antipathetic to him. He had never been properly informed about the first negotiations, and had come to regard him as a dangerous, mercurial being who must be kept in strict subjection: when the relief expedition was authorised, he insisted on his being put formally under Wolseley and his powers limited to the Khartoum neighbourhood. How could one who thought in flashes be understood by one who thought in paragraphs! As for the dervish army, drunk with blood and dreams of Paradise, he seems to have envisaged it as a collection of dark-skinned Midlothian radicals.

Such were the limitations of the man – a great man. The tragedy lay in the fact that, being what he was, he was faced with a task in which his weaknesses became clamant and his virtues silent. But he should not be left to bear the blame alone. Lord Northbrook, when disaster came, nobly resolved never to serve under him again. It would have been more to his credit if this resolve had come earlier, and if the old man had been brought to reason by those colleagues who lacked his faults, as they assuredly lacked his genius.

# ACT THE FOURTH:
# THE RACE AGAINST TIME

## I

Ill-luck dogged from the start the expedition thus tardily sanctioned. There was a delay of a fortnight before the Nile route, which Wolseley favoured and on which some preliminary work had been done, was finally approved. Sir Frederick Stephenson, commanding the British troops in Egypt, preferred the Suakim-Berber road, but he had argued against it in March, and the objection to it had been increased by the loss of Berber. Wolseley, with his Red River campaign in mind, desired to follow the same methods, with Canadian flat-bottomed boats and Canadian boat-men, and these took time to collect. He had a series of difficult cataracts to pass, and, since food could not be obtained locally, he must carry supplies for a hundred days. He was determined to leave nothing to chance, and the transport of 7000 men in such a terrain required elaborate preparations. Bases were established along the river, and at Dongola an advance guard was stationed, the nucleus of a flying column, the Camel Corps, which was to strike across the Bayuda desert from Korti to Metemmah, thereby cutting off the great bend of the river. These advance troops were intended to enter Khartoum, and hold it till the rest of the army arrived, when the relief and evacuation could be completed.

Wolseley was a competent soldier, and his deep friendship for

Gordon – the two men remembered each other every night in their prayers – gave him the most urgent motive for speed. But it was his custom to make war disposedly, taking all due precautions, and he was not the man for a swift and hazardous enterprise. From Suakim to Berber the distance was 250 miles; from Cairo to Khartoum it was 1000 miles as the crow flies, and 1650 miles if the river were followed. If it was to be a race against time for Gordon's life, the Nile route seemed impossibly slow, especially when the nature of the flotilla was remembered – steamers which, in Lord Charles Beresford's words, 'had the appearance of a boat and the manners of a kangaroo,' which leaked at every rivet and whose boilers 'roared like a camel.' There was a younger soldier, Sir Frederick Roberts, who five years before had made a brilliant dash to Kandahar; had he been given the task with Indian troops he might have crossed the desert from Suakim and have been in Khartoum in November. Mr Chamberlain, who knew nothing of the art of war but had often an uncanny *flair*, would have put the little-known Major Kitchener in command of a flying force. But though part of Wolseley's delay came from his too meticulous methods, the purpose of his enterprise involved elaboration. For it was not a hussar-ride for the rescue of one man or a handful of men, but for the evacuation of a multitude. Nothing less would fulfil Britain's pledge, and nothing less would Gordon accept. To succeed, any relieving force must hold the river and stave off the Mahdi for many months.

On September 27 Wolseley left Cairo. On October 5 he was at Wadi Halfa, where he established a temporary base and spent a month in supervising the transport. There he heard of the disaster to the *Abbas*, but he was not yet greatly alarmed about the situation in Khartoum. He was busy organising the Camel Corps in four regiments, two of cavalry, one of the Guards, and one of mounted infantry, with a detachment of Royal Marines, and he could not expect it to be ready to leave Korti for the desert journey much before the end of the year. He arrived at Dongola on November 3, and on November 17 received a message from

Gordon, which gave some account of the Khartoum position, advised the crossing of the desert to Metemmah, and promised that four of his steamers would be waiting there. The message contained these significant words: 'We can hold out 40 days with ease; after that it will be difficult.' Since the letter was dated November 4, this meant that by December 14 the position would be grave. But Gordon's friends were always confident that he could better his best, and that if he spoke of holding on for six weeks he could hold on for six months. The concentration at Korti could not be completed before Christmas, and the crossing of the desert and the advance to Khartoum would take at the best a fortnight. That is to say, Gordon could not be rescued till six weeks or more after the last date which he had given as his limit of endurance.

Still Wolseley does not seem to have been specially anxious; at any rate he took no steps to expedite the pace of his movements. Slowly with immense labour the flotilla struggled up the river through the rapids from Wadi Halfa to New Dongola, from New Dongola to Old Dongola and open water, from Old Dongola to Korti. Wolseley was well behind his time, and his original hope of spending Christmas in Khartoum had gone. By December 15 only the advance guard was at Korti, and it was not till a fortnight later that the concentration there was completed. The Commander-in-Chief proceeded to divide his forces. The Nile Column, 3000 men under General Earle, should continue up the river, deal with Berber, and at Metemmah join the Desert Column, which was to strike direct across the Bayuda wastes.

At 3 o'clock on the afternoon of December 30 the latter force rode out of Korti, a little over a thousand strong, under the command of Sir Herbert Stewart, with Major Kitchener to lead the way. The same day an Arab brought a message from Gordon, a twist of paper dated December 14, with the words 'Khartoum all right.' But he brought also a verbal message: 'We are besieged on three sides. Fighting goes on day and night... Bring plenty of troops if you can... Food we still have is little – some grain and biscuit. We want you to come quickly. You should come by Metemmah or Berber. Make by these two roads. Do not leave Berber in your rear.' These words made Wolseley realise the gravity of the situation, but they also convinced him that he must not go direct in force to Khartoum, but must first take Berber. That might be a slow business, including the passing of two cataracts, and it was not till the bend at Abu Hamed was reached that the boats could get the favouring north wind. The one hope of speed lay in Sir Herbert Stewart and his camelry, now cut loose from their base and launched into the desert.

## II

Meantime during the last three months of the year Gordon was fighting his desperate battle against odds, and he was fighting it alone. He had no confidant except his journal, and no counsellor except the valour of his heart. On the technical side his resistance was an astonishing feat. With 7000 inferior troops he had to defend a wide periphery against twenty times their number of intrepid fanatics. Within his defence zone he had a multitude of scared civilians, who had to be fed and comforted. He was short of food, and had to scrape it together and deal it out like gold dust. He was short of ammunition and guns, while the besiegers had ample supplies. The contemptuous message which Wad-el-Nejumi sent him on September 12 was a fair picture of the Mahdi's army. 'One man of them in battle is better than a thousand of you. He has provided us with weapons of war, in which thou thinkest there is victory, with Krupp cannons, with mountain guns for battle, in which thou shalt taste of evil, if thou turn aside from the way of God.' Moreover Gordon had to keep the river open down to Shendi and Metemmah for the relief expedition which was his only hope. Up and down the falling Nile plied his penny-steamers, getting fuel from the banks when and where they could, running the gauntlet of a ceaseless bombardment, the only link with the outer world, except the occasional Arab spies who bore Major Kitchener's messages to the beleaguered city.

As the days passed Gordon found his tools breaking in his hand. There were few men whom he could trust. Officers neglected their duties, and stole the soldiers' rations; there were plots to blow up the magazine and to betray the city; there was a perpetual purloining of grain. He had to keep his eye on every detail of the defence work or it would be scamped. In such circumstances he had to rule largely by terror, and his punishments were instant and severe. Often he repented of his severity, for he detested harshness, but there was no other way. The shivering townspeople clung to his skirts, supplicated him, cursed him, blessed him. He had to drive them with a light rein, for they were on the near edge of panic.

So he encouraged them with announcements of the speedy arrival of British troops, and assurances that he would not fail them. 'Know,' he declared on November 26, 'that if Mohammed Ahmed should call me for three years to surrender Khartoum, I will not listen to him, but will protect your wives and families and possessions with all energy and steadfastness.' He had a band to play every Thursday on the palace roof – boys, for the men were all in the trenches – and when the palace was bombarded he directed that it should be kept brilliantly lit up to show his scorn of the enemy. Such *panache* was the only chance of keeping civilian spirit from cracking. 'When God was portioning out fear to all the people in the world,' he told Bordeini the merchant, 'at last it came to my turn, and there was no fear left to give me. Go tell all the people in Khartoum that Gordon fears nothing, for God hath created him without fear.'

Yet he jumped when a shell dropped near him, and had to remind himself that 'judicious bobbing' under fire was permissible. We can learn from his journal that his nerves were stretched to the last limit with overwork, anxiety, and hope deferred. He was no doubt impatient and sometimes unjust, but another man would have gone mad. He vented in writing his grievances against Baring and Granville and all that world which was daily growing dimmer, and then set himself patiently to the realities of his task. Sometimes he had strange fancies. He heard that the Mahdi had a French prisoner and decided that it must be Ernest Renan, whom he had met once in London. He wanted to meet Renan again; Renan had not, like Slatin, betrayed his Lord, for he had been always an unbeliever. He thought much of death, and decided that, if the city fell, he would not blow up the palace and perish with it – that would be too like suicide; he would let himself be taken and, if called upon, die a martyr to the faith. Sometimes he was sustained by the conviction that his defence had been rather a fine thing – at least as good as Sebastopol. Not that he thought much of fame – 'if we analyse human glory, it is composed of nine-tenths twaddle, perhaps ninety-nine hundredths twaddle.' But his professional pride was not quite forgotten. What might he not have done, he asked himself, if he had only had trusty troops whom he could use for counter-attacks 'in a real siege with no civil population or robbers of officers'?

The Moslem year begins on Trafalgar Day. The Mahdi had his new year's text from the Koran: 'Victory from God, conquest is at hand.' He sent one last summons to surrender, and Gordon's reply was, 'I am here like iron... It is impossible for me to have any more words with Mohammed Ahmed – only lead.' November compelled him to revise his old view of the poor quality of the dervish troops, for on the 14th came a terrific Arab attack on the fort of Omdurman on the west bank of the White Nile. The place was sturdily defended, but the enemy succeeded in cutting the fortified lines which connected it with the river and thereby isolating it. Unless the English came soon Omdurman must fall, and that would mean the end of Khartoum. But the Arabs did not at once press their advantage. They established a battery at Khojali across the Blue Nile, from which at a range of a mile and a quarter they bombarded the palace. One unpleasant result was that his few steamers were in constant danger.

Sunday, December 14, was the last of the forty days which Gordon had given Wolseley as the limit of his power to hold on. On that day he made the last entry in his journal:

Now mark this, if the Expeditionary Force, and I ask for no more than two hundred men, does not come in ten days, the town may fall; and I have done my best for the honour of my country. Goodbye. C G GORDON.

On the 15th the little *Bordein* set off down the river, with the journal, and letters, official and private. Among the latter was one to his sister Augusta, which had this postscript 'I am quite happy, thank God, and, like Lawrence, I have tried to do my duty.'

### III

Between Korti and Metemmah lay 176 miles of desert. The route had been surveyed by Ismail for a railway, and the Desert Column had his map to guide them. Since the enemy was known to be near it was necessary to establish supply posts and to leave guards at the few waterholes. The scarcity of camels prevented the expedition from making the whole journey at once, and it was decided to establish an advanced base at the wells of Jakdul, 98 miles off, and return for the rest of the troops and supplies. This double journey was the first delay.

Riding through nights of brilliant moonlight the column reached the Jakdul wells, three deep pools in the clefts of the black hills, on the morning of January 2. It had been on the march for sixty-four hours with only four hours of sleep. There the Guards battalion was left as garrison, and the rest returned to Korti. It was not till January 8 that Sir Herbert Stewart set out again, with his strength now increased to 1600 British troops, 300 camp-followers, and some 2400 camels and horses. He had also part of the Naval Brigade under Lord Charles Beresford, which was intended to man the steamers believed to be waiting at Metemmah. On the 12th Stewart reached Jakdul, where he found all quiet, and on the 13th resumed his advance. Nine days had been occupied by the double journey.

Meanwhile the Mahdi's picked troops, whom the delay had amply warned of the British movements, were hastening north to bar the way. When on the evening of the 16th Stewart reached the ridge which looked down on the wells of Abu Klea, he saw 10,000 dervishes encamped beneath him. The night was made hideous by the beating of their war drums, but there was no attack. On the morning of the 17th the British advanced in a square, which presently halted when it was seen that the Arabs were moving forward. Inside the square were the camels and the ammunition; it stood in the trough of a little valley, with the enemy in front and on the adjoining hills. Suddenly on its rear appeared a cluster of green and white flags, and 5000 dervishes swept down upon the Heavy Camel Regiment and the Naval Brigade, 'an immense surging wave of white-slashed black forms brandishing bright spears and long flashing swords.'

What followed was a second Inkerman, a soldiers' battle. For such fighting the Arabs were as well equipped as the British, and they had the fury of their wild faith to nerve them. Stewart's troops had the wretched Gardner gun, which perpetually jammed in action. They had the old Martini-Henry rifle, which also jammed, while the Arab Remington, using a different kind of cartridge, was free from this fault. Against the razor-edged Arab spears were pitted blunt bayonets and cutlasses that bent and twisted. In physical strength and weapon power, as in numbers, the British were hopelessly outmatched. They were saved only by their steady, disciplined courage. The enemy broke into the rear of the square and pressed his assault up to the camels, which stopped his rush and gave the front and flanks time to face inwards. For a little there was a desperate hand-to-hand struggle, officers and men fighting side by side. No Arab emerged from that broken square, and at length the enemy withdrew leaving over 1000 dead on the field. But the British had paid a heavy price for their victory, for out of their little force they had lost 18 officers and 158 other ranks. Worse still, Colonel Burnaby, whom Wolseley had destined to take charge at Metemmah, lay dead after all his journeyings, 'slain in the desert by a wandering spear.'

Abu Klea had involved another day's delay. That night Stewart bivouacked by the wells, his men without food or blankets. Next day, the 18th, the march was resumed in the afternoon, and continued through the night, till early on the morning of the 19th, the column came in sight of the Nile. It halted for a brief rest, and once again the enemy drew round it in clouds. A zariba was hastily formed, and breakfast was eaten under a rain of bullets. Stewart received a wound which proved to be fatal, and the command devolved upon Sir Charles Wilson, a distinguished intelligence officer who had never before commanded troops in the field. The new leader decided to press on to the Nile, and the square moved slowly forward, sweeping the dervish force before it by its deadly fire. The sun set, the twilight deepened to dusk, and under a young moon the British came to the river bank. The troops who had been marching and fighting for four days without sleep and with little food or water, and had lost one man in ten, could at last drink and rest, but so weary were they that, when they came back from quenching their thirst at the river, they fell down like logs.

Next day was occupied in fortifying their position, and on Wednesday the 21st Sir Charles Wilson advanced against Metemmah. The attack had not begun when four steamers, flying the Egyptian flag, were seen to be coming from the south. They were Gordon's steamers; the troops broke into cheers, and there was a rush to the river bank to welcome them.

The march through the Bayuda desert had been a splendid feat of arms, but it had been slow, and there was no man in the column whose thoughts were not reaching beyond his present troubles to what might have happened, or be happening, a hundred miles up those blue waters to whose shores he had fought his way. The last word from Gordon had left Khartoum on December 14, and its appeal had been urgent. It was now thirty-eight days since then – the 21st of January.

71

# ACT THE FIFTH: THE END

Abu Klea was fought on January 17, and the news of it brought consternation to the Mahdi's camp. The sword of the infidel had proved more potent than the sword of the Prophet. A salute of 101 guns was ordered on January 20 to proclaim a victory, but this was only to delude the people of Khartoum, for in the camp itself there was lamentation. Gordon on that day saw through his telescope a multitude of weeping women and guessed the truth, and presently a spy confirmed it. Mohammed Ahmed called a council of his emirs, and all but one urged a retreat to El Obeid and the raising of the siege. 'If one Englishman,' they argued, 'has kept us at bay for a year, how much more will these thousands of English, who have defeated our bravest men at Abu Klea, be able to crush us and drive away.' Only Abd-el-Kerim stood out; let them attack Khartoum at once, he said, and there would still be time to fall back if they failed.

For a day or two the dervish council hesitated. News came of another victory of the English and their advance to the Nile bank. The sight of a dozen redcoats would have sent the whole army westward into the desert. But the 21st passed and the Mahdi's scouts reported no British movement, nor on the 22nd or the 23rd. The courage of the dervishes revived and their temper hardened. When at last on the 24th news came that the British were advancing, Abd-el-Kerim's views had prevailed, and it was resolved forthwith to attack the city. Abu Klea had been misrepresented; the infidels were in doubt and fear, for if they had been victorious they would long before have reached Khartoum.

On January 15 Omdurman had capitulated to the enemy, and he was now able to plant guns on the west bank of the White Nile and double the fury of his bombardment. More serious, the river was falling fast, and the trenches and ramparts on the west side of the lines, abutting on the stream, had to be pushed further into the drying mud. But with the loss of Omdurman this became impossible. The river was ceasing to be a defence, and presently it had receded so far that a sand ridge appeared some 300 yards from the east bank. If the enemy landed on this he had only to wade through a shallow lagoon to be inside the lines. A spy carried this news to the Mahdi's camp.

When Gordon wrote the last words in his journal on December 14 he closed his account with the outer world. After that date we have only the fragmentary evidence of the survivors of the garrison, and of prisoners in the dervish camp. By the end of the year the state of the city was desperate indeed. There was no food ration left to issue at the close of the second week of January. Gum was served out and the pith of date trees, and for the rest the food was lean donkeys and dogs and rats. Dysentery was rife, and the soldiers on the ramparts were almost too weak to stand, their legs swollen, and their bodies distended by gum and water. The spirit had gone out of the stoutest, and even Faragh Pasha advised surrender. But Gordon was adamant. He suffered those civilians who desired it to go to the Mahdi, and many went, but he would permit no weakening in his council of notables. Resistance must be maintained to the end. The news of Abu Klea had for a moment given hope, and he issued daily announcements that the British were coming, would arrive any hour. But when no smoke appeared on the northern horizon the last dregs of resolution were drained from the sick and starving people. 'They will no longer believe me,' he told Bordeini. 'I can do nothing more.' But he did not relax his efforts. Day and night he was on the ramparts, in the streets, in the hospitals, the one vital thing in a place of death and despair.

We have no journal to tell us his thoughts, but we can guess them from the nature of the man. He had become two beings – one ceaselessly busy in his hopeless duties, scanning the distances anxiously for the smoke which would mean relief; the other calm and at ease. On the palace roof at night with the vault of stars above him he found that union with the Eternal which was peace. His life had always hung as loosely about him as an outworn garment, and now the world of space and time had become only a shadow. 'I would,' he had once written to his sister, 'that all could look on death as a cheerful friend, who takes us from a world of trial to our true home.' The communion with the unseen which had been the purpose of all his days was now as much a part of him as the breath he drew. Like the ancient votaries of the Great Mother, he had passed through the bath of blood and was *renatus in aeternum*. His soul was already with the congregation of the firstborn.

The letters which Gordon's steamers brought to Gubat on the 21st were dated December 14 and their tone was sufficiently grave. Ten days' time was given as the extreme limit of resistance. There was another message on a scrap of paper: 'Khartoum all right. Could hold out for years'; but this was clearly meant as a device to deceive the enemy, should it fall into his hands. Sir Charles Wilson had no illusions about the need for haste, but his experience had not lain in the leading of men, and his was not the character for bold and decisive action.

Stewart's instructions from Wolseley had been to take Metemmah, which would serve as a base later for the River Column, and to send Wilson on to Khartoum in Gordon's steamers, accompanied by Lord Charles Beresford and part of the Naval Brigade. Wilson now found himself in command of the whole force, and he hesitated about his next duty. When he received Gordon's papers it is clear that he should at once have gone himself, or sent someone, to Khartoum. As it was, he delayed three days in spite of the protests of Gordon's Arab emissaries. The reason is obscure, but it is probable that Beresford was the cause. He was ill at the moment, suffering from desert boils, and he was eager to accompany the relief force, as he had been instructed. News came of an enemy advance from the south, and then of another from the north, and he induced Wilson to use the steamers to make reconnaissances in both directions, in the hope, doubtless, that he would presently be fit for duty. Two and a half days were wasted in a meaningless task.

This delay was the last and the most tragic of the tricks of fate. Had Burnaby lived it is certain that a steamer would have set out for Khartoum on the afternoon of the 21st. Had that been done, it is as certain as such things can be that Gordon would have been saved. It was not till the 24th that the Mahdi decided upon an assault, and it was not till the evening of the 25th that the details were agreed upon. Allowing for the difficulties of the journey, the steamers, had they left on the 21st, would have been in time to convince the hesitating dervishes, and turn them against Abd-el-Kerim's plan; they might even have been in time had they left on the 22nd. This was the view of the Europeans in the Mahdi's camp who were in the best position to know – of Slatin and of Father Ohrwalder. 'Had twenty redcoats arrived in Khartoum,' the latter has written, 'it would have been saved... If the English had appeared any time before he delivered the attack, he would have raised the siege and retired... Many survivors have said to me "Had we seen one Englishman, we should have been saved." ' By such a narrow margin did a great enterprise fail.

Wilson eventually set out on the morning of Saturday the 24th, in two steamers with twenty British soldiers and a few bluejackets – all the troops, at Gordon's request, being clad in scarlet tunics. Misfortune dogged his path. On the evening of the 25th the *Bordein* struck a rock in the Sixth Cataract, which caused a delay of twenty-four hours. Early on the 27th the Shablukah gorge was passed, and that day the voyage continued under heavy rifle fire from both banks. There were Arab cries from the shore that Khartoum had fallen, but they were not believed. Early on Wednesday the 28th, the expedition came in sight of Khartoum beyond the trees on Tuti island, and ran the gauntlet of the batteries at Halfaya. Then they opened the palace and saw through glasses that no flag was flying. The channel at Tuti was one long alley of rifle fire. As they rounded the corner they beheld a wrecked city, with the Mahdi's banners flaunting under the walls, and knew that all was over. They were sixty hours too late.

Wilson could only turn and retreat. The little gimcrack steamers had a perilous journey. Both were wrecked and in danger of capture, and a young officer of the 60th, Stuart-Wortley, set out alone in a boat for Gubat to bring help. On February 1 at dawn Beresford was hailed by a voice from the river, which could only stammer, 'Gordon is killed... Khartoum has fallen.' From Gubat the news crossed the desert, and was flashed to a world which for months had drawn its breath in suspense. Queen Victoria at this, as at most times, was the voice of her people. 'She went to my cottage, a quarter of a mile off,' her private secretary wrote to Baring, 'walked into the room, pale and trembling, and said to my wife, who was terrified at her appearance, "Too late !"'

All day on Sunday the 25th there was a movement of Arab troops to the east bank of the White Nile. Wad-el-Nejumi, the commander of the storm-troops, had his camp at Kalakala, a mile south of the defences. That evening, as twilight fell, a boat put off from the western shore, and four figures joined him and his emirs; it was Mohammed Ahmed himself with his three khalifas. The Mahdi blessed the troops and gave them his orders. In the name of God and the Prophet he bade them attack Khartoum in the dark of the night; let them have no fear, for those who fell would go straight to Paradise. The four returned as silently as they had come, and Wad-el-Nejumi unfolded his plans.

One part of the force should attack the western half of the defences, breaking through the gap which the falling river had left on the shore side. The second division should attack on the east between the Messalamieh Gate and Buri, but if the western assault succeeded this section was to hold its hand, side-step to the left, and follow the first division. In front would go the skirmishers, then the main force of spears and swords, and then further riflemen, with the cavalry in reserve on the rear flanks. Bedsteads and bundles of straw were carried to fill up the trenches, if necessary. The Mahdi had left no precautions untaken, for he was nervous about a direct assault, though his emirs had assured him that God had made their path easy and plain.

As soon as the moon set the movement began. In silence the left division crept towards the defences. Now they were at the ramparts, and at that moment a fierce bombardment broke out from every Arab gun around the city. Under this cover it was easy for the left flank of the attack to break through the gap at the river bank, which only three armed barges defended. In a few minutes they were inside the lines, sweeping to the east, and taking the rest of the defences in rear. Swiftly they crossed the space between the lines and Khartoum, a space dotted with cemeteries, magazines and slaughterhouses, and bore down on the helpless city. The post at the Messalamieh Gate, finding its position turned, was compelled to fall back, and through that gate poured the contingent destined for the Buri attack. By four o'clock Khartoum had fallen, and the siege of three hundred and seventeen days was over. Most of the attackers made for the streets and the business of plunder and massacre. But one body, with whom there were no emirs, rushed to the palace, and swarmed in at the garden entrance.

Of Gordon's last doings our accounts are few and bare. It appears that he had spent the day indoors, striving to put resolution into his notables, but in the evening he had examined part of the defences. From the palace roof he had his last search for the steamers that never came. He had seen the Arabs crossing the White Nile and may have guessed what was afoot, for he did not go to bed. The sound of musketry and guns after midnight told him of the attack, but he could do nothing. The end had come, and he was in the hands of God.

The firing drew nearer, and then he heard that dreadful sound which strikes terror into the boldest heart, savage men baying like hounds for lust and blood. Presently there came a tumult in the garden, and the death cries of his black sentries. He walked to the head of the staircase, dressed in a white uniform, with a sword at his belt, and a revolver in his right hand. The darkness was passing, and the first crimson of dawn was in the sky.

He saw a mob of dark faces and bright spears, and with them no high officer. That he knew meant instant death. Not for him to be taken prisoner and confronted with the Mahdi, with the choice before him of recusancy or martyrdom. He must have welcomed the knowledge. He stood, his left hand resting on his sword-hilt, peering forward as was his fashion. An Arab – Mohammed Nebawi was his name; he fell at the battle of Omdurman – rushed on him, crying 'O cursed one, your time has come,' and struck at him with his spear. Gordon did not defend himself. He turned away with a gesture of contempt, and in a second a dozen spears were in his body, and men were slashing at him with their swords. The hour of his death was about 5.30, when it was almost full dawn.

His slayers cut off his head, and brought it in triumph to the Mahdi's camp. Mohammed Ahmed had wished him to be taken alive, but he bowed to the will of Allah. It was now broad day, and the captive Slatin, sick and anxious, crawled to his tent door. He found a group of shouting slaves, carrying something wrapped in a bloody cloth. They undid the cloth and revealed the head of Gordon, his blue eyes half opened and his hair as white as wool.

'Is not this,' cried one, 'the head of your uncle the unbeliever?'

'What of it?' said Slatin. 'A brave soldier who fell at his post. Happy is he to have fallen; his sufferings are over.'

# EPILOGUE

The policy of Britain contained the germ of its own reversal. Gordon's prophecy was true; if there was to be peace on the lower Nile the upper river must be controlled. The white-clad figure fronting the dervish spears at sunrise on that January morning was more persuasive in his death than in his life. Wisely the first step was backward. The Soudan was evacuated, and steadily Egypt gathered her forces for the recoil. A succession of devoted British officers drilled the Khedive's troops into an army. At Ginniss, between Wadi Halfa and Dongola, towards the end of 1885 Sir Frederick Stephenson defeated the dervish forces, and thereby warded off the invasion of Egypt proper. In 1889, at Toski, Sir Francis Grenfell fought the opening battle under the forward policy; there Wad-el-Nejumi fell. He blooded the new Egyptian army, and gave it its first taste of self-respect. Two years later Osman Digna was defeated at Tokar, and the eastern Soudan was tranquillised.

In those years Egypt, fortunately for her, was forgotten by Britain, but under the major of sappers, who had been the chief link with Gordon, she was quietly and surely preparing her own salvation. In 1897 the final advance began. The railway was pushed on from Wadi Halfa to Abu Hamed. In April 1898 Sir Herbert Kitchener by his victory at the Atbara laid open the road to Khartoum. Five months later the battle of Omdurman, fought beside the Mahdi's yellow, pointed tomb, broke for good and all the power of the fanatics who for fifteen years had burdened the country. A more economical triumph was never won, for the cost of the conquest of the Soudan was only 60 British and 160 Egyptian lives, and a sum of £2,350,000, far less than that of the relief expedition which failed. In 1884 Kitchener had calculated that 20,000 British troops would be needed for the task; his judgment was sound, for at Omdurman he had 22,000. Baring, now Lord Cromer, had nothing to do but, in his own words, 'abstain from a mischievous activity and act as a check on the interference of others.' Mr Balfour telegraphed on the eve of the Atbara, 'The Sirdar may count upon the support of Her Majesty's Government whichever course he decides on adopting. Unless he wishes for a military opinion, we refrain from offering any remarks which would interfere with his absolute discretion.' A far cry from the waverings of Lord Granville!

Kitchener was hailed by Cambridge, when he received his doctor's degree, as '*Gordonis ultor.*' But Omdurman was no mere punitive act, and Gordon needed no avenger. The drama of Khartoum was more than a strife of common interests and passions; it was a clash of opposing worlds, of fervent creeds, of things not intrinsically base which could not dwell side by side in the compromise which we call civilisation. Tragedy sprang more out of rival greatnesses than out of rival follies, and it was dignified by the quality of the actors. If it revealed human weakness and perversity, it revealed – and not on one side alone – the faith and courage which ennoble our mortality. The end, as in all great tragedies, was peace – the Gordon College in Khartoum, a just law for all, protection for the weak, bread for the hungry, square miles of tillage where once the Baggara raided... In 1919 the son of the Mahdi offered his father's sword to the British king as a token of his fealty. The old unhappy things had become far off and forgotten.

# BIBLIOGRAPHICAL NOTE

The principal authorities for Gordon's life are *The Journals of Major-General C G Gordon at Khartoum* (1885) and *Letters of General Gordon to his Sister* (1888); the British Official White Paper on China (1864) and the Blue Books on Egyptian Affairs (1884-5). The telegrams in the last-mentioned are not always given in full, but the originals are in the Record Office, and have been printed by Mr Bernard M Allen in his *Gordon and the Sudan* (1931). Additional material in the shape of letters and reports will be found in *Sudan Notes and Records*, vols. x. and xiii.

The early Lives (by D C Boulger, 1896; A E Hake, 1884, 1896) were apt to be uncritical eulogies. The best account of Gordon's work in Africa is that by B M Allen cited above, which is supplemented by his *Gordon in China* (1933). Lytton Strachey's ingenious travesty will be found in his *Eminent Victorians* (1918). An illuminating imaginary conversation between Gordon and Gladstone is in H D Traill's *The New Lucian* (1900). Mr H E Wortham's *Gordon: an Intimate Study* (1933) is a vivid and judicial sketch of the whole career, and makes use of many hitherto unpublished letters.

The best narrative of the Mahdi's rising is Sir Reginald Wingate's *Mahdism and the Egyptian Sudan* (1891). Useful too are Sir Rudolf Slatin's *Fire and Sword in the Sudan* (1906) and Father Ohrwalder's *Ten Tears' Captivity in the Mahdi's Camp* (1903).

The story of the Relief Expedition is told in Lord Edward Gleichen's *With the Camel Corps up the Nile* (1886), Sir W F Butler's *The Campaign of the Cataracts* (1887), Sir Charles Wilson's *From Korti to Khartoum* (1886), the opening chapters of Mr Winston Churchill's *The River War* (1899), and Lord Charles Beresford's *Memoirs* (1914).

Gordon appears in every biography and autobiography of the time. The most valuable are Lord Cromer, *Modern Egypt* (1908); Sir George Arthur, *Lord Kitchener* (1920); Sir F D Maurice and G C A Arthur, *Lord Wolseley* (1920); Vetch, *Life of Lt.-Gen. Sir Gerald Graham* (1901); John Morley, *Life...of Gladstone* (1903); Bernard Holland, *Life of the 8th Duke of Devonshire* (1911); Wemyss Reid, *Life of W E Forster* (1888); Fitzmaurice, *Life of Earl Granville* (1905); Garvin, *Life of Joseph Chamberlain*, vol. ii. (1933); and Buckle, *Life and Letters of Queen Victoria*, vol. iii. (1928).

# John Buchan

## Julius Caesar

John Buchan wrote of Caesar 'He performed the greatest constructive task ever achieved by human hands. He drew the habitable earth into an empire which lasted for five centuries, and he laid the foundations of a fabric of law and government which is still standing after two thousand years.'

In this romantic biography Buchan attempts to understand the hidden thoughts of the great soldier. He charts the tale of Caesar's youth, early political career, success, conquest of Gaul and of the world, ending with his murder at the hands of Brutus and the Republican-minded conspirators.

## Grey Weather

Grey Weather is the first collection of sketches from John Buchan, author of *The Thirty-nine Steps*. The subtitle, Moorland Tales of My Own People, sets the theme of these fourteen stories. Shepherds, farmers, herdsmen and poachers are Buchan's subjects and his love for the hills and the lochs shines through.

# John Buchan

## Oliver Cromwell

John Buchan sets out to redress popular opinion of this English soldier and statesman. His biography achieves that aim, starting with Cromwell's childhood and youth.

Born in 1599, Cromwell was a devout Puritan who, when war broke out, formed his Ironsides. He won the battles of Marston Moor and Naseby and brought Charles I to trial. After establishing the Commonwealth, he suppressed the Levellers, Ireland and the Scots. In 1653, five years before his death, he established a Protectorate.

John Buchan wrote of Cromwell 'He is a soldier now on the grand scale, strategist as well as tactician, statesman as well as fighting man, and it is by this new phase of his military career that his place is to be adjudged in the hierarchy of the great captains'.

## The King's Grace

This sympathetic portrait starts with the death of Edward VII and George V's succession. It was a reign that saw many changes including the Union of South Africa, the First World War and the General Strike of 1926.

John Buchan wrote that 'This book is not a biography of King George, but an attempt to provide a picture – and some slight interpretation – of his reign, with the Throne as the continuing thing through an epoch of unprecedented change.'

# John Buchan

## Montrose

This is a compassionate biography of the legendary Scottish commander, James Graham, Marquis of Montrose. John Buchan describes Montrose's command of the royalist forces during the 1644 to 1650 war with the Covenanters. Montrose's exceptional strength, leadership and military genius are brought to life. Buchan also illustrates an important period in Scottish history, adding his own measure of adventure to this study.

## The Clearing House

This anthology of extracts from Buchan's writings is well worth reading for its historical range and wide selection of subjects close to the author's heart. Alongside portraits of Julius Caesar, Cleopatra, Virgil, Cromwell and Sir Walter Scott, to name but five, are lyrical descriptions of landscapes. Buchan's love for the great outdoors comes to the fore in his account of the African veld and in the more domestic *Wood, Sea and Hill*. There are also short essays on fishing, shooting and golf, among other sports.

52148815R00055

Made in the USA
San Bernardino, CA
05 September 2019